Foyle's Philavery

A Treasury of *Unusual* Words

Collected by Christopher Foyle

Chambers

Chambers

An imprint of Chambers Harrap Publishers Ltd
7 Hopetoun Crescent
Edinburgh, EH7 4AY

First published by Chambers Harrap Publishers Ltd 2007

Reprinted 2007 (three times)

A CIP catalogue record for this book is available from the British Library.

ISBN 978 0550 10329 1

Editors: Vicy Aldus, Ian Brookes, Hilary Marsden
Prepress Controller: Becky Pickard

Designed and typeset by Chambers Harrap Publishers Ltd, Edinburgh
Printed and bound by Clays Ltd, St Ives plc

Introduction

Philavery /fil-*a*-vuh-ri/ *n* an idiosyncratic collection of
uncommon and pleasing words

I first began to collect words which I considered to be of 'uncommon usage' at the time of the first Gulf War in 1990 after the US commander, General Norman Schwarzkopf, described information which he considered to be of little or no value as 'bovine scatology'. Although I was familiar with the word 'bovine', I had to refer to the dictionary to discover the meaning of 'scatology'.

From then on, I started to make a note of any words I came across that I was unfamiliar with, or that I was unfamiliar with in a specific context, and checked their meaning in a dictionary. This 'collection' of words, which would eventually evolve into *Foyle's Philavery*, grew rapidly; to these previously unknown words I added new gems – pleasing, interesting and unusual words, both ancient and modern, which attracted my attention in some way and demanded to be remembered.

From archaic words like 'Fastingong' and 'hebberman' which are all but lost to modern ears, to dialect terms such as 'beek' or 'sniddle' which, if not lost already, may soon suffer the same fate, literally hundreds of words came to be recorded. Some particularly evocative words like 'afflatus' or 'crepuscular' effortlessly conjured up vivid images; playful words with interesting and amusing sounds like 'funambulist', 'fabiform' or 'pungy' lingered in my memory. I came across words both well- and little-known which, like 'halcyon' and 'ultracrepidarian', had fascinating and often surprising etymologies. Some uncommon words seemed quite simply to provide a more satisfying and evocative alternative to their more familiar counterparts – 'amanuensis' for secretary, 'murken' for darken, or 'crapulent' for hung over.

My words are found in a wide variety of places. I take six newspapers a day: five British broadsheets and the *International Herald Tribune*.

Having read the news in one of them, I skim the news pages of the others and mostly concentrate on the editorials, letters, opinions and comments sections. These, together with *The Economist*, *The Spectator* and specialist periodicals on my various other interests, provide a steady stream of unusual words – at least, unusual to me.

I have not read much fiction since the early 1970s, not because I have lost my enjoyment of it, but because my interest in a wide range of subjects – principally archaeology, ancient civilizations and the origin of races, history, current affairs, travel and topography, aviation, genealogy and parapsychology – take up much of my time. As it is, family, social and business commitments, together with my compulsive newspaper-reading, leave less time than I would like for reading the books that collect in piles by my bed and which I dip into most evenings.

My passion for reading began early. As a young child I quickly became an avid reader. This was hardly surprising as books and reading pervaded my life from birth, my entire family being steeped in the book trade. My grandfather, William Foyle, was the co-founder of Foyles bookshop in Charing Cross Road in London, and my father, Richard Foyle, and one of his sisters, my aunt Christina, followed him into the business; my mother worked for a company producing illustrated books.

In my teens I read *Exploration Fawcett*, based on the diaries of Colonel Percy Fawcett, an eccentric Englishman who tramped through the jungles and mountains of South America in the early 20th century at the behest of the Royal Geographical Society to map, and so help define, the boundaries between a number of South American countries. In the course of his eight expeditions, Fawcett became interested in the legends of the people he encountered; tales of lost cities and of a white race which pre-dated the first Spanish conquerors. These accounts sparked in me an interest in the anthropology, archaeology and pre-history of South and Central America, which subsequently extended to cover other regions and civilizations, interests which remain an abiding passion to this day.

I followed my parents into the book trade, training first in the family firm and subsequently spending three years in Europe. This whetted my appetite for travel but, bookselling not being particularly well paid, it was difficult to indulge that appetite, or my yen to learn to fly, until a career switch into financial services generated the requisite funds. Flying developed my interest in topography, the ability to 'read' a landscape and its features being an important part of navigating in a small plane as well as a useful skill in archaeology, and flying also laid the foundations of my subsequent aviation businesses.

In 1999, life came full circle with my appointment as director and then chairman of the Foyles book business on the death of my aunt. It is satisfying to be following in the footsteps of earlier generations of Foyles, but it has one drawback – easy access to so many books has swelled the piles of books, and subsequent philavery-bound cuttings, around my house and office to almost unmanageable proportions!

I hope you will find the journey around the words listed here as fascinating, intriguing and inspiring as I have.

Christopher Foyle
November 2006

Acknowledgements

I would like to acknowledge the help of Linda McCash, my PA at Air Foyle, who typed and consolidated the original list of words as I discovered them; my editor Hilary Marsden for her additional research and for fleshing out my original ideas; Christine Jelleyman, my mother-in-law and a demon at Scrabble, who came up with the word *philavery* when we were discussing an appropriate title; and my wife Catherine who puts up with my spending vast amounts of time on this and many other curricular and extra-curricular activities.

Note on pronunciations

Part of the enjoyment of collecting unusual words is going on to use them in everyday conversation. Where the pronunciation of a word is not immediately obvious, guidance is included in the note accompanying the entry. Although these notes should be fairly self-explanatory, a list of the letter-combinations used to indicate the different vowel sounds is included below:

a	as in *bat*
ah	as in *far*
ai	as in *mine*
aw	as in *all*
ay	as in *pay*
e	as in *pet*
ee	as in *tee*
i	as in *bid*
o	as in *got*
oh	as in *note*
oo	as in *moon*
ow	as in *house*
oy	as in *boy*
u	as in *bud*
uh	as in *the* (unstressed)
ur	as in *bird*
yoo	as in *tube*

Aa

abacinate

verb

to blind someone by putting red hot metal before their eyes

     The word occurs in many dictionaries but I can find no recorded uses of it in a text apart from the lyrics of the 1986 song 'Angel of Death' by American thrash metal band Slayer.

abactinal

adjective

(of radiate animals) located on the side or end of the body opposite to where the mouth is found

abada

noun

a rhinoceros

     This name was used in the 16th and 17th centuries, and appears to be derived via Portuguese from an Asian or Arabic word.

abaiser

noun

a former name for 'animal black', a black pigment made from burnt animal bones or ivory and used in paints and engraving inks

     The word is pronounced 'uh-*bay*-suh', rhyming with 'chaser'.

abalienate
verb
1 (in civil law) to transfer a title to something from one person to another; to alienate
2 to estrange
3 to cause mental aberration

abbatial
adjective
relating to an abbey, abbot or abbess
> I take a particular interest in words relating to abbeys since I am lucky enough to live in a beautiful 12th-century abbey set deep in the Essex countryside. Since the building has been in domestic use since the time of the Reformation, the reminders of former abbots and abbesses are purely architectural, although the heart of Saint Roger Niger, Bishop of London from 1229 to 1241, is reputedly buried here, and is yet to be found.

ablactation
noun
1 the process of ceasing to secrete milk
2 the weaning of a child off its mother's milk and onto solid food

ablation
noun
1 the loss or removal of material from a body by surgery, or from a physical feature by erosion, evaporation, melting, weathering, etc
2 the deliberate removal of surface material from a spacecraft caused by friction when re-entering the atmosphere

abligurition
noun
extravagant expenditure on food and drink

abnegate
verb
1 to deny oneself something; to give up a right or privilege
2 to renounce or abjure

abrin
noun
a deadly poison found in the seeds of the plant *Abrus precatorius*
 ও The hard, bright red seeds of *Abrus precatorius* (more commonly
   known as Jequirity, Black-eyed Susan, Crab's Eye, Indian Liquorice or
   Rosary Pea) are often used as ornamental beads or within percussion
   instruments. Despite these innocuous uses, the deadly toxin abrin – a
   protein found within the seeds' hard outer shell – is closely related
   to, although more potent than, ricin. The name of the genus *Abrus* is
   derived from the Greek *habros* meaning 'graceful'.

absumption
verb
a process of gradual consumption; wasting away

abthane
noun
1 an abbacy or abbotric
2 secular jurisdiction over property formerly belonging to an abbey
 ও Derived via Latin from Gaelic *abdhaine*, meaning 'abbacy', the origin
   of this Lowland Scots word was lost and a false etymology arose
   assigning the meaning 'a superior thane' to the word.

acarologist
noun
someone who studies mites and ticks

accrete
verb
1 to grow together; to form around or on something
2 to attract (such growth)

acephalic
adjective
1 having no head; headless
2 having no chief or leader
 ও The word is pronounced 'ay-sef-*al*-ik', with the stress on the third
   syllable.

acerebral
adjective
1 having no brain
2 lacking intelligence or intellectual abilities
&ᴥ The word is pronounced 'ay-suh-*reeb*-rul', with the stress on the third
syllable.

acetabulum
noun
1 (in anatomy) the cup-shaped socket of the hip bone into which the
head of the thigh bone fits
2 (in insects) the cavity in the thorax into which a leg fits
3 (in some inveterbrates, such as tapeworms) a cup-shaped sucker
&ᴥ This term is derived from the Latin *acetabulum* meaning 'vinegar cup',
a cup-shaped vessel of metal or ceramic used for holding vinegar at
table. As if to prove the ubiquity and importance of this humble cruet,
in time the word also came to express a measure (roughly 2½ fluid
ounces) as well as the scientific terms above. It is pronounced 'as-et-*ab*-
yoo-lum', with the stress on the third syllable.

acidulous
adjective
1 slightly sour in taste
2 rather sharp or caustic in speech

acolaust
noun
a person who enjoys indulging in sensual pleasures; a sensualist

acouchy
noun
a small rodent, *Dasyproctidae acouchy*, that is related to the agouti
and lives in the Amazonian rainforest

acoupe
verb
to accuse; to blame

acrasial
adjective
excessive; intemperate; irregular; disordered

acroasis
noun
a discourse that is intended to be heard rather than read; a talk, lecture or sermon

acrophobia
noun
an abnormal fear of heights or high places

acrosome
noun
a cap-like structure over the head of a sperm cell which produces the enzymes that enable a sperm to penetrate an egg
  ঽ The word is derived from the Greek words *akron*, meaning 'end', and *soma*, meaning 'body'.

acrostic
noun
a poem or other literary composition or a word puzzle in which certain letters in each line, taken in order, form a word or phrase
  ঽ Derived from the Greek words *akron* 'end' and *stichos* 'a line of verse', the word first appears in English in the 1500s, although the concept is well-known from classical antiquity. The earliest use of acrostics is reputed to be within the cryptic prophesies of the Sibyl of Erythraea. She was one of several prophetesses linked with the god Apollo, who during frenzies inspired by the god would reveal prophecies or answer questions. The Sibyl is purported to have delivered her messages in the form of acrostics written on leaves. The practice of creating acrostics lives on today in the form of wordgames and puzzles, and as creative exercises given to young children.

actinal
adjective
(of radiate animals) relating to or located on the side of the body where the mouth is found or from which the tentacles radiate

adamantine
adjective
1 extremely hard, resistant to penetration
2 stubborn, resistant to persuasion

adipous or adipose
adjective
fatty; related to or characterized by fat, especially fat stored in body tissues

adjuvant
adjective
1 helpful; ancillary
2 (in medicine) enhancing or aiding the effect of a treatment

adonize
verb
to beautify or adorn oneself
    ॐ This verb is appropriately derived from the mythological character Adonis, a beautiful youth loved by the Greek goddess Aphrodite. The word is derived via Latin and Greek from Phoenician *adon*, meaning 'lord'.

adumbrate
verb
1 to indicate, describe or represent an outline of something
2 to foreshadow
3 to overshadow
    ॐ This word is derived from Latin *adumbrare* meaning 'to shade in or sketch'. The root of the word, the Latin term *umbra* meaning 'shade or shadow', is shared by 'sombre', 'umbrage' and 'umbrella'.

adventitious
adjective
1 accidental, unintentional, occurring by chance
2 (in biology) indicating something formed accidentally or in an unusual position

advowson

noun

(in English ecclesiastical law) the right to nominate a member of the Anglican clergy for a vacant benefice, or the right to make the appointment

> ࿂ The word is pronounced 'ad-*vow*-zun', with the stress on the second syllable.

aedicule

noun

(in architecture)

1 a doorway, window frame or niche in a wall treated as if it were a building, eg by framing the opening with flanking columns, a pediment, etc

2 a miniature reproduction of a larger feature of a structure for ornamental purposes

> ࿂ The word is derived from Latin *aedicula* meaning 'a small house or room'.

afflatus

noun

inspiration, especially a divinely inspired creative impulse

> ࿂ The word is derived from Latin *afflare* 'to breathe on', conjuring up a gloriously literal image for the ancient concept of divine inspiration. It is pronounced 'uh-*flay*-tus', with the stress on the second syllable.

agonic

adjective

having or making no angle

agriology

noun

the description or study of the customs of primitive peoples

agrypnia

noun

1 wakefulness, sleeplessness

2 a vigil before certain church festivals, especially in the Greek Orthodox Church

    ટ♥ The word is pronounced 'ag-*rip*-nee-uh', with the stress on the second
    syllable.

agterskot
noun
a final payment for a crop, wool clip, etc, made to its members by a
farmers' co-operative society or similar body, being the difference
between the total amount due to them and the advance payment
already received
    ટ♥ The word is derived from Afrikaans *agter* meaning 'after' and
    (*voor*)*skot* meaning 'payment'.

ailurophobia
noun
an abnormal fear of cats

aleatory or aleatoric
adjective
1 depending on chance or uncertain contingencies (as in an aleatory
contract)
2 (in music) involving the random choice of notes by the performer
    ટ♥ This word, reflecting the principles of randomness, appropriately takes
    its derivation from Latin *aleator*, meaning 'dice-player', from *alea*, 'a die'.

alembroth
noun
an obsolete term for mercury ammonium chloride, used as a flux for
metals
    ટ♥ The origins of this evocative word are, disappointingly, unknown. Also
    known as 'sal alembroth', it was believed by alchemists to be the 'salt of
    wisdom'.

Algol
noun
1 the second brightest star in the constellation Perseus, an eclipsing
binary also called *Beta Persei*
2 a high-level computer programming language that uses algorithms,
mainly for solving mathematical and scientific problems

› The name of the variable star Algol is believed to be derived from Arabic *al ghul* meaning 'demon' or 'mischief-maker', suggesting that Arab scholars may have been aware of the waxing and waning of the star's light even before the invention of the telescope. The second meaning of Algol is less romantically derived from *Algo*rithmic *l*anguage.

alliaceous
adjective
relating to plants of the *Allium* genus (which includes onions, leeks, garlic and chives) and particularly their taste or smell

allograph
noun
1 a variant shape of a letter, eg in different typefaces or handwriting
2 a letter or group of letters that represents a particular sound
3 handwriting, especially the signature, of one person written down by another

allopathy
noun
the treatment of disease with remedies that have an opposite effect to the symptoms (the opposite of homeopathy)

alopecia
noun
the partial or complete absence of hair from parts of the body where it usually grows, as a result of old age (eg baldness) or disease

› The word is derived from a Greek word *alopekia*, which has the suprising meaning of 'fox-mange'.

alpargata or alpargate
noun
a type of sandal or light canvas shoe with a plaited fibre sole; an espadrille

› The word is pronounced 'ahl-pah-*gah*-tah', with the stress on the third syllable.

alphameric
adjective
consisting of letters and words; containing alphabetical, numerical and other symbols
> ৫ The word is a variant of the more familiar 'alphanumeric'.

alula
noun
a group of small feathers that grows on the first digit of the wing of some birds
> ৫ This pleasing little word is a diminutive of the Latin *ala* meaning 'wing' and refers to the point on modern birds' wings which corresponds with a mammal's thumb. This flight-control device is also, less pleasingly, known as a 'bastard' or 'spurious' wing.

amanuensis
noun
a secretary, or more usually a literary assistant, who writes from dictation or copies manuscripts
> ৫ A pretty, musical-sounding word which is derived from Latin *servus a manus* 'servant at handwriting' and the ending *-ensis* 'belonging to'. Despite the reference to 'servants' and 'belonging' it is a word which reminds me of my efficient, trustworthy and utterly indispensable secretaries, and one which I would like to see brought back to wider use.

amatorious
adjective
amatory; relating to sexual love or desire

anabiosis
noun
1 (in biology) a state of suspended animation or greatly reduced metabolic activity in which vital signs become imperceptible
2 revival from such a deathlike condition
> ৫ Although I find this a useful term to describe the lethargic tendencies of certain teenagers of my acquaintance, its proper use refers to a more useful state of suspended animation – one into which some animals and

plants fall, enabling them to survive long periods of extreme temperatures or drought. The word is derived from Greek *ana* 'up or back' and *bios* 'life'.

anadromous
adjective
(of fish) swimming up rivers from the sea in order to spawn in fresh water
  ও The word is pronounced 'an-*ad*-ruh-mus', with the stress on the second syllable.

anbury or amburry
noun
1 a spongy tumour or wart on horses or oxen
2 a disease affecting the roots of turnips

ancona
noun
an altarpiece, usually consisting of several pictures or painted panels connected by an architectural structure, such as a frame

androconium
noun
one of the scales on the wings of certain male moths and butterflies which emits a smell attractive to females of the species

andrology
noun
the branch of medicine specializing in men's health, especially urological problems and the reproductive system

anemotropism
noun
movement or growth in response to wind and air currents
  ও The word is derived from Greek *anemos* 'wind' and *tropos* 'turning'.

anenterous
adjective
(in zoology) lacking a stomach or intestine

angelet
noun
a small gold coin equivalent to half an angel
   ও The angelet circulated in England and subsequently in Britain from the late 15th century until the early 17th century. The angel coin was so called because its inscription showed the archangel Saint Michael slaying a dragon. It is pronounced '*ayn*-juh-lit', with the stress on the first syllable.

annelid
noun
types of inveterbrates, such as earthworms, leeches, etc, that have long, soft bodies made up of ring-like segments

anthropogeny
noun
the study of the origin or evolution of the human race
   ও The word is derived from Greek *anthropos* 'human being' and *genesis* 'development'.

anthropophagy
noun
the practice of eating human flesh; cannibalism

antigropelos
noun
waterproof leggings or gaiters worn to protect the legs or clothes
   ও The word was originally a proprietary name for the garment and is said to be derived from Greek *anti* 'against', *hygros* 'wet' and *pelos* 'mud'.

antipyretic
noun
a drug that prevents or reduces fever
adjective
relating to a drug that has this effect

apert
adjective
open; unconcealed; undisguised; public
adverb
openly; publicly

aphasia
noun
a loss of or reduction in the ability to speak or to understand the spoken or written word owing to damage to the brain, eg from a stroke
> The word is derived from Greek *aphatos* 'speechless'.

aphelion
noun
the point in the orbit of a planet or comet when it is furthest from the Sun

aphorism
noun
1 a pithy and often witty saying which expresses a truth or opinion
2 a brief statement of a principle in any science
> The word is derived from Greek *aphorizein*, meaning 'to define'.

apogamy
noun
reproduction which occurs without the usual sexual process taking place, eg in ferns

apogee
noun
1 (in astronomy) the point in the orbit of a body, such as the Moon, when it is furthest from the Earth
2 the greatest height or most distant point, eg in the trajectory of a missile

apophatic

adjective

(in theology) relating to the belief that God cannot be known and can be described only in terms of what he is not

apophthegm or apothegm

noun

a short saying or maxim, possibly even pithier than an aphorism

&ε The word is pronounced '*ap*-oh-them', with the stress on the first syllable.

aporia

noun

1 a figure of speech expressing doubt
2 an insoluble difficulty in the meaning of a text

&ε The word is derived from Greek *aporos* 'impassable'.

aposiopesis

noun

(in rhetoric) a sudden stop in and failure to complete a thought or sentence

apostasy

noun

the renunciation or rejection of a religious belief, moral principle or political affiliation that someone had previously held

Apotactite

noun

a member of a sect of early Christians who renounced all their possessions

apotheosis

noun

1 the act of raising someone to divine status; deification
2 the glorification of someone or something that embodies an ideal

Appaloosa
noun
a North American breed of horse which is usually white or grey, with
a pattern of dark spots
> The name 'Appaloosa' is said to derive from the Palouse Indian tribe,
> who lived in the valley of the River Palouse in Washington and Idaho,
> and were renowned for their breed of distinctive spotted horses. There
> are nine basic Appaloosa coat patterns with beautifully evocative
> names, from 'frosted hip' and 'spotted blanket' to 'snowflake' and
> 'marble'.

aproctous
adjective
(in zoology) lacking an anus

aproneer
noun
a 17th-century London slang word for a shopkeeper or tradesman
> The word was used pejoratively of the Parliamentarians during the
> English Civil Wars.

aprosexia
noun
an abnormal inability to pay attention, often characterized by a lack
of interest in anything
> Another term which to me sounds like it was invented for use by
> parents of some teenage children.

araponga or arapunga
noun
the campanero or South American bell-bird

arcifinious
adjective
having a frontier that forms a natural defence

aril
noun
a sac-like fleshy covering of some seeds, often brightly coloured

aristate
adjective
1 (in botany) having pointed, beard-like appendages, like some grains and grasses
2 (in zoology) having a slender, sharp or spine-like tip

aristology
noun
the art or science of cooking and dining
    ह✒ This word is gloriously derived from Greek *ariston* 'breakfast or lunch' and *logos* 'study'. Usage dates from the early 19th century but the term has been largely superseded by 'gastronomy'.

ascesis
noun
the habitual practice of self-discipline; asceticism
    ह✒ The word is pronounced 'uh-*see*-sis', with the stress on the second syllable.

ashplant
noun
a walking stick or a whip or goad made with a sapling from an ash tree

assilag or assailag
noun
a storm petrel
    ह✒ This dialect name is derived from Gaelic and means 'storm' or 'cold, sharp blast', and is also applied to constant, restless motion.

astragal
noun
1 a small circular moulding, either plain or carved, around the top or bottom of a pillar
2 (in Scottish architecture) a glazing bar

asymptotic
adjective
pertaining to two items that approach one another without ever meeting or intersecting

atavistic
adjective
1 relating to or resembling remote ancestors rather than parents
2 reverting to an earlier type

attap
noun
any type of palm leaf used to thatch the roofs of buildings in southeast Asia

aulic
noun
a ceremony observed when conferring a doctorate of divinity at some universities, and the subsequent disputation
adjective
1 relating to a royal court, especially one of the two supreme courts of the Holy Roman Emperor in Germany prior to 1806
2 courtly; ceremonious

auricula
noun
1 (in biology) the external ear, or something shaped like an ear lobe
2 (in botany) a central European species of primula, *Primula auricula*
3 (in medicine) a conical pouch projecting from the top of each atrium of the heart
  ❧ The *Primula auricula* is also commonly known as 'Bear's ear' because of the shape of its leaves.

auspicate
verb
1 to presage, indicate by signs, omens, etc
2 to begin or inaugurate something in a way calculated to bring good luck

ॐ The word is derived from Latin *auspicari*, from *auspex* 'observer of birds'.

autochthon
noun
1 one of the original or earliest known inhabitants of a country or region; an aborigine
2 a plant or animal indigenous to a specific country or region

autumny
adjective
relating to or typical of autumn

avodire
noun
a tree of the Mahogany family, and the pale, smooth tropical hardwood obtained from it

axiopisty
noun
the quality that makes something worthy of trust

azeotrope
noun
(in chemistry) a mixture of liquids which boils at a constant temperature without the composition of the components changing
ॐ This term is derived from the Greek *a-* 'not', *zeein* 'to boil' and *tropos* 'turning'.

Bb

badinage
noun
talk that is humorous, playful, bantering

baldric or baldrick
noun
1 a broad belt or sash worn around the waist or hung from one shoulder diagonally across the body to hold a sword, bugle, etc
2 the zodiac
    ∾ The term 'baldric' has been used for years by military historians, and is indeed known to have originated in the 14th century. Despite this long and illustrious history, it is practically impossible for contemporary observers to think of the word without picturing the faithful, turnip-loving servant of Edmund Blackadder in the BBC television series.

balladromic
adjective
(of missiles etc) maintaining course towards a target
    ∾ This misleadingly tuneful word which at first reading conjures up images of ballets or singsongs has, in reality, a far more unromantic definition which rather brings to mind recent world events.

bandoline
noun
1 a sticky, strongly scented ointment used for dressing hair
2 an unidentified musical instrument, possibly a mandolin

ह The musical instrument gave its name to a clavier piece by Couperin and 'The Bandoline Player', one of the *Bab Ballads* by librettist W S Gilbert (of Gilbert and Sullivan fame).

barnet
noun
the hair; the head

ह Barnet, in Hertfordshire, now a London borough, was the site of a famous horse fair, and 'Barnet Fair' became Cockney rhyming slang for 'hair'.

barratry
noun
1 the offence of habitually instigating lawsuits, especially groundless ones; vexatious litigation
2 (in marine law) a breach of duty, through fraud or criminal negligence, by a ship's master or crew that results in injury or loss to the ship's owner
3 the sale or purchase of ecclesiastical offices or offices of state

barton
noun
1 a farmyard
2 the lands of a manor retained for the use of the lord and not let out to tenants

ह The word is derived from Old English *bere*, meaning 'barley', and *tún*, meaning 'enclosure'.

bascule
noun
1 an apparatus that acts like a lever, with one end rising as the other sinks
2 a type of bridge whose roadway section is raised and lowered using counterweights; a type of drawbridge

ह Despite the somewhat uninspiring nature of the definition, I was drawn to this word because of its pleasing sound and its rather neat etymology – it is derived from the French word for a see-saw.

basial
adjective
relating to kissing
 › The word also has a more mundane existence as a variant spelling of 'basal', meaning 'relating to or located at the base of something'.

basto
noun
the ace of clubs in the card games quadrille and ombre

bathetic or bathotic
adjective
1 (in speech or writing) characterised by bathos, ie a sudden and usually unintentional change from the important, serious or beautiful to the ordinary, trivial or absurd
2 anticlimactic

bathybius
noun
a name given to a gelatinous substance found in mud dredged from the floor of the Atlantic Ocean
 › The discoverer of the substance, the 19th-century biologist T H Huxley, thought it was primordial matter and as such a source of all organic life. He had to admit his mistake when the substance was found to be the product of a chemical reaction between the mud and the preservative solution in which it had been stored.

batterfang
verb
to attack with the fists or nails; to beat and claw at
 › This delightfully descriptive word's origins are obscure, although it is thought to derive from northern English dialect.

battology
noun
an excessive and pointless repetition of words in speaking or writing

bavardage

noun
idle chatter
 ঌ The word is taken from the French, meaning 'talking, verbiage'.

beal

noun
(in medicine) a pustule or boil
verb
to suppurate; to fester

bedizen

verb
to ornament or dress up in a gaudy and tasteless manner
 ঌ The word is pronounced 'bid-*ai*-zun', rhyming with 'horizon'.

beek

verb
1 to warm, to make comfortable
2 to bask in the warmth of the sun or a fire
 ঌ I find this an enchanting word, both as a sound and a concept, and
 would love to see it brought back into common use. Derived from Old
 Scandinavian *beke* or *beek* meaning 'to expose the body to warmth' it
 recalls pleasant pastimes such as baking and basking, and conjures up
 images of cosy sitting rooms, roaring fires and long, hot summer holidays.

behemoth

noun
1 something that is unusually large or powerful
2 an enormous animal, possibly a hippopotamus, described in the
book of Job in the Bible
 ঌ The word is Middle English, derived from the Hebrew for 'beast',
 which might itself derive from the Eygptian for 'water-ox'.

bellibone

noun
a woman of exceptional beauty and goodness
 ঌ The word is derived from French *belle et bonne* 'beautiful and good'.

belluine

adjective
1 relating to or like a beast
2 brutal

bellwether

noun
1 the leading sheep in a flock, so-called because it usually has a bell around its neck
2 a contemptuous term for a ringleader whose lead is followed in an unquestioning, sheep-like fashion

belomancy or bolomancy

noun
a form of divination using arrows marked with symbols or questions, guidance being sought by firing the arrows or drawing them at random from a bag or quiver

  ᔰ The word is derived from Greek *belos* 'dart' and *manteia* 'divination'.

bema

noun
a ceremonial platform in an assembly

  ᔰ Originally used of the praesidium of the Athenian political assembly, the term has come to mean the raised platform in a synagogue from which services are conducted and the area around the altar in Orthodox Christian churches.

berbice chair

noun
a reclining armchair with long arm rests, the lower parts of which can be swivelled inwards to act as foot rests

  ᔰ This type of chair is named after Berbice, a river and county in Guyana.

berm

noun
1 a narrow strip of grassland or pathway beside a road, canal or embankment, etc

2 (in military fortifications) a narrow ledge between a ditch and the base of a parapet

beshrew
verb
to wish harm to; to invoke evil on; to curse

bident
noun
1 an instrument or weapon with two prongs
2 a two-year-old sheep

bield
noun
shelter, refuge, protection; a place or person providing shelter or refuge
verb
to protect, shelter, cover; to take shelter
adjective
sheltered

> ॐ This is a Scots word, variously spelt 'bield', 'beild', 'beel', ''beeld', 'biel' or 'beil', which is derived ultimately from an Old English word meaning 'boldness'.

bifer
noun
a plant that bears fruit or flowers twice a year

> ॐ The word is pronounced '*bai*-fuh', rhyming with 'cypher'.

biffin
noun
a variety of dark red cooking apple, particularly common in Norfolk

> ॐ A wonderful little word which brings home the enormous wealth and variety of English apples which have been all but lost to modern society. According to the East of England Apples and Orchards Project, although three quarters of Norfolk's orchards have been grubbed up in the last 50 years, and at least 30 varieties of apples native to the county have been lost, some 40 local varieties still remain, glorying in names such as Winter Majetin, Herbert Eastoe and Jordan's Weeping. Biffin would appear to be the local dialect pronunciation of 'beefing', which

was given to the apple because of its deep red colour. It was also the name of a dessert of baked apples of this variety, popular in Victorian times.

biggin
noun
1 a tight-fitting cap tied under the chin, usually worn by children or as a nightcap by men
2 a coffee pot
> ᚹ The coffee pot, an 18th-century forerunner of the percolator, was named after its inventor, George Biggin.

birl
verb
1 to revolve rapidly; to whirl round; to dance
2 to cause something to spin rapidly, eg a coin

birse
verb
1 to bruise or cause injury by pressure, especially the pressure of a crowd
2 to press, especially in a crowd
noun
1 a bruise; pressure
2 a struggle to resist pressure
> ᚹ This is a Scots word derived from Old English *brysan* 'to crush'.

birsle
verb
to scorch; to warm thoroughly; to toast
> ᚹ Another Scots word, which was also used in northern England in earlier centuries.

blabagogy
noun
a criminal environment
> ᚹ The word is included in *Mrs Byrne's Dictionary of Unusual, Obscure and Preposterous Words* by Josefa Byrne, and is much quoted on the Internet, although I have not been able to track it down in any other dictionaries.

blennophobia
noun
an abnormal fear of slime or mucous

> ટ⚭ One of the pleasures of collecting unusual words is the occasional uncovering of a term for which I had not previously suspected there was any need at all. 'Blennophobia' has now officially gone to the top of my list of fascinating phobias, alongside 'bibliophobia' (fear of books), 'euphobia' (fear of good news), 'Francophobia' (fear of France) and 'symmetrophobia' (fear of symmetry).

blowen
noun
a prostitute; a courtesan

> ટ⚭ This is a cant word – an example of the specialized jargon used by thieves to prevent others from understanding their conversations.

blurt
noun
an explosive emission of breath from the mouth, usually to express contempt
verb
to say something abruptly, tactlessly or without thinking of the effect or result

bodacious
adjective
1 remarkable; prodigious
2 bold, audacious, unconventional

bodle
noun
a small copper coin issued in Scotland in the 17th century and worth about one-sixth of an English penny

Boeotian
adjective
1 relating to the region, people or dialect of Boeotia, the region of ancient Greece to the north-west of Attica

2 dull, boorish, ignorant, lacking in culture

ॐ The second meaning arose because of the disdainful attitude of Athenians towards their rural northern neighbours, whom they regarded as country bumpkins.

bollimong or bullimong

noun

a mixture of different grains (often oats, peas and vetches) grown together as a forage crop for cattle

bombilate

verb

to make a sound by rapid vibration; to buzz

bongrace

noun

a bonnet with a projecting peak or a hat with a wide brim, worn to protect the complexion

ॐ The word is pronounced '*bon*-grays', with the stress on the first syllable.

bongre

adverb

with good will; agreeably

ॐ The word is pronounced '*bon*-gray', with the stress on the first syllable. It is derived from the French *de bon gré* 'of good will'.

boose

noun

a stall for a cow, ox, horse or other animal

bor

noun

neighbour; boy

ॐ An East Anglian dialect form of address, derived from the Old English *bur* or *gebur* meaning 'neighbour', which is still in common use. It is perhaps best known from the songs of unlikely Sixties pop star The Singing Postman, whose extraordinary hit 'Hev Yew Gotta Loight Bor' knocked The Beatles from the top of the East Anglian charts in

1965, and who at the height of his fame appeared on *Top of the Pops* alongside the Rolling Stones.

borak or borack

noun

1 banter

2 ridicule

> ๑๏ This is an Australian and New Zealand slang word derived from an Australian Aboriginal term meaning 'no' or 'not'.

borborygmus

noun

(in medicine) the rumbling sound of gas and fluid in the intestines

> ๑๏ A wonderfully formal word to use to describe a delightfully basic bodily function. It is pronounced 'baw-buh-*rig*-mus', with the stress on the third syllable.

bordrage or bodrage

noun

a raid, a border incursion

boreas

noun

a wind from the north, named after Boreas, the god of the north wind in Greek mythology

bosky

adjective

1 consisting of or having an abundance of bushes, shrubs or trees; wooded, bushy

2 tipsy, on the point of becoming drunk

bothan

noun

a house where alcohol is consumed without a licence or duty being paid on the liquor; a shebeen

> ๑๏ This Scots word originates from the Gaelic term for a hut or shack and is related to the more familiar word 'bothy'.

botling or bottlin

noun

a fish also known as a chub or chevin

bottomry

noun

(in maritime law) a contract whereby a ship and its cargo are used as security for a loan to finance a voyage

> ॐ Under this sort of contract, perhaps inevitably also known as 'bummery', the loan is repaid if the ship arrives safely but if it sinks, the lender loses his money.

boudin

noun

(in French and Cajun cuisine) a highly seasoned sausage or black pudding, made of pork

> ॐ The word is derived from Old French *bodine* meaning 'intestines'. It has also given its name to the official march of the French Foreign Legion, 'Le Boudin', as *boudin* is a colloquialism for the red blanket roll that tops the backpacks of Legionnaires.

bouleversement

noun

1 a reversal; a complete overthrow

2 a tumult; a violent uproar

> ॐ The word is derived from Old French *bouleverser* meaning 'to overturn'.

bourdon

noun

1 the bass stop in an organ or harmonium

2 the lowest bell in a ring of bells

3 the drone pipe of a bagpipe

> ॐ The word derives from French, meaning 'a humming tone'. In medieval times it could also mean a low voice or undersong accompanying the voice singing a melody.

bovarism

noun

an unreal or romanticized perception of oneself; a preoccupation with such a perception

> ৯৺ This word is of course derived from Emma Bovary, the dreamy protagonist of Gustave Flaubert's influential realist novel, *Madame Bovary*. Born and raised in rural Normandy, Emma's love of popular novels creates within her an obsession with the luxury and glamour of high society. Her deluded yearnings for a romantically idealised and ultimately unattainable existence lead her into a spiral of adultery and debt which eventually cause her downfall.

brachistochrone

noun

a curve between two points that is covered in a shorter time by a body moving along it than any other curve

brad

noun

a thin, flat nail whose head is the same width or only slightly wider than the rest of the nail

> ৯৺ The word is derived from Old Norse *broddr* meaning 'spike'.

bradypepsy or bradypepsia

noun

slow digestion

bragget

noun

an alcoholic drink made by fermenting ale and honey with spices etc

bragly

adverb

in a manner to be bragged of; finely; proudly

brandade

noun

a Provençal dish made from salted cod

> ☙ The word is derived via French from Provençal *brandado*, which means 'a thing that has been shaken'.

brane

noun

1 (in physics) an extended object with a number of given dimensions, eg one-brane

2 (in brane cosmology) an object similar to our four-dimensional universe which moves in a space-time of higher dimension

bratticing

noun

1 wooden boarding, often temporary, used to partition off something dangerous, eg machinery, or to divide or line a mine shaft

2 a wooden breastwork erected for protection during a siege

breastsummer

noun

(in architecture) a horizontal beam or girder across a broad opening, supporting the superstructure of a building's wall; a long lintel

bredie

noun

(in South Africa) a stew of meat and vegetables

brimborion

noun

a thing with no value or use; trash; nonsense

brodekin

noun

a buskin or half-boot

broggle
verb
to fish, especially for eels, by thrusting a sharp stick with bait on it into holes in the river bed

brool
noun
a deep, low humming sound; a murmur, as of a large crowd

browet
noun
a soup or broth made with the juice of boiled meat
 {※ The word is pronounced '*brow*-it', rhyming with 'allow it'.

bruit
noun
a report or rumour
verb
to spread or report news, rumours, etc
 {※ The word is derived from French, meaning 'noise', from the verb *bruire* 'to roar'.

Bucentaur
noun
the state barge of the doges of Venice, from which the doge performed the annual Ascension Day ceremony of wedding Venice to the sea
 {※ Despite the apparent link with a mythical creature, half man and half ox, known as the bucentaur, the name of the barge is known to have derived from Venetian *buzino d'oro* 'golden barge', which was Latinized as *bucentaurus*.

buckram
noun
cotton or linen cloth stiffened with gum or paste and used as an interfacing in the lining of clothes, or in bookbinding
 {※ The word came into Middle English from Anglo-French *bukeram*; it might derive ultimately from the city of Bokhara (now Bukhara in modern Uzbekistan), then noted for its cloths.

bumbass
noun
1 a projectile thrown by a bombard
2 a musical instrument with a single string stretched over a bladder and played with a bow

bunco or bunko
noun
a confidence trick or swindle, especially by card-sharping
verb
to swindle or cheat
> ஜ This is North American slang which might be derived from Spanish *banca*, a type of card game.

bundobust or bandobast
noun
organization, a system or discipline
> ஜ The word is derived from Hindi and Persian words meaning 'tying and binding'.

bungo
noun
a kind of canoe or barge used in Central and South America; a small boat used in the southern parts of the USA

byssus
noun
1 a tuft of strong silky filaments by which certain molluscs make themselves fast to rocks etc
2 a fine linen fabric made in ancient times
> ஜ This word is derived from Greek *byssos* meaning 'linen' or 'flax' but originates in ancient Egypt, where the fabric was used to wrap mummies.

Cc

caballine
adjective
of or relating to a horse; equine

cabotinage
noun
behaviour typical of a second-rate actor or strolling player, implying a tendency to play to the gallery or overact

cacafuego or **cacafogo**
noun
a spitfire; a braggart
　　❧ This word is derived from the name of a Spanish galleon *Cacofuego* captured by Sir Francis Drake. The literal Spanish meaning is 'shit fire' but it was translated euphemistically into English as 'spitfire'.

cacoëpy
noun
the mispronunciation of words
　　❧ The word is derived from Greek *kakos* meaning 'bad' and *epos* 'a word'. It is pronounced 'kak-*oh*-uh-pi', with the stress on the second syllable.

cacolet
noun
a chair, litter, etc, fitted to the back or pack saddle of a mule for

carrying travellers in mountainous terrain, or to transport the sick and wounded of an army

cacoon
noun
the hard round seed of the tropical climber *Entada scandens*, about two inches in diameter, which is used for making purses, boxes, etc

caduceus
noun
1 (in the ancient world) a herald's wand or staff, such as that carried by Hermes or Mercury
2 a symbol of the medical profession, and of commerce, modelled on Hermes' winged staff entwined by two serpents

 ꤮ The word is Latin, derived from Greek *karykeion*, from *karyx* 'herald'. It is pronounced 'kad-*yoo*-si-us', with the stress on the second syllable. The caduceus represented power, peace, wisdom and prosperity and was carried by several ancient deities including the Egyptian god Anubis and the Babylonian goddess Ishtar. The staff of Asclepius, the Greek god of healing, is often used interchangeably with the caduceus as a symbol for the medical profession. It depicts a rod entwined by a single snake, connected in ancient times with the process of healing and rebirth.

cagnotte
noun
(in certain gambling games) the proportion of a stake reserved for the bank; a kitty

calefacient
noun
something that produces a sensation of heat when applied to the body
adjective
warming

callipygian
adjective
having buttocks that are beautifully proportioned or finely developed

ཨ༔ This pleasingly apposite and beautiful-sounding word is, appropriately enough, borrowed from an epithet of Aphrodite, the Greek goddess of love, beauty and desire. *Kallipygos*, from *kallos* 'beauty' and *pyge* 'buttock', is one of the more charming sobriquets of the goddess – many others were applied to her, referring to her various habits, haunts and attributes, including *Tymborychos* 'the grave digger', *Nikephoros* 'bringer of victory' and *Pandemos* 'lover of all people'. (Whether this final epithet refers to her position as goddess of love, or her famously abundant amorous exploits is unclear.)

canard
noun
1 a false rumour or story
2 a extra wing fitted to the front of an aircraft to provide greater stability or control

ཨ༔ The word is French for 'duck' and also 'hoax', from Old French *caner* 'to quack'.

candicant
adjective
growing white; whitish

cannikin or canikin
noun
a small can, sometimes used as a drinking vessel

canophilia
noun
a love of dogs

capitulary
noun
1 a member of a cathedral or other chapter
2 an ordinance, or a collection of ordinances, such as those of the Emperor Charlemagne and his successors

captious
adjective
inclined to find fault or raise trivial objections
> ࣷ The word is derived from Latin *captiosus* 'arguing falsely'.

cark
verb
to worry or to be burdened with worries
> ࣷ The word is derived via Norman French from the Latin *carricare* 'to load'.

carnaptious
adjective
irritable; quick-tempered; quarrelsome; cantankerous
> ࣷ The word is found in Scottish and Northern Irish usage and also, as 'knaptious', in Cumbrian dialect.

carom or carrom
verb
to collide and rebound off something
noun
a shot in billiards in which the cue ball strikes two balls in succession, now known as a cannon
> ࣷ The word is derived from the French *carambole*, meaning 'a stroke in billiards'. The word is still in everyday use in the USA.

cassie
noun
1 a basket made of straw or woven heather, grass, rushes, etc
2 a pavement, or a paving stone
> ࣷ The first sense of this Scots word, most common in the Orkneys, is derived from Icelandic *kassi* or *kass* 'basket, box'. The second sense is a variant form of 'causeway'.

cassine
noun
a farmhouse that has been turned into a military post to prevent the advance of enemy forces

casuistry
noun
clever but fallacious reasoning used to make a case, resolve a problem or argument, etc, often making the morally wrong seem acceptable

catamite
noun
a boy in a sexual relationship with a man
  ᚼ The word is derived via Latin from the Greek name *Ganymede*, the boy seduced by the god Zeus in Greek mythology. It was originally applied to the younger partner in a relationship between two men in the ancient world, especially in Greece.

cataphatic
adjective
(in theology) relating to the belief that God has provided enough evidence of his nature to be known to humans positively and affirmatively

catchpole
noun
(in medieval England) a sheriff's officer, especially one responsible for arresting debtors and recovering outstanding debts
  ᚼ If medieval tenants were unable to pay their taxes in cash, then goods, usually poultry, were seized in lieu. The word is derived from old forms of French and Provençal meaning 'chase fowl', and was used particularly in Norfolk and Dorset.

cautel
noun
1 craftiness, trickery; a deceit or stratagem
2 caution; a precaution
3 a direction for the correct administration of the sacraments in the Roman Catholic Mass
  ᚼ The word is derived via French from Latin *cavere* meaning 'to beware, to take care'.

caveach
verb
to pickle mackerel or other fish according to a method used in the West Indies
ₑ The word is pronounced 'kuh-*veech*', rhyming with 'teach'.

cavendish
noun
tobacco that is pressed into solid cakes, softened and fermented
ₑ The term applies to the process of curing and method of cutting the tobacco rather than the type of tobacco.

cavil
verb
to make trivial objections to something
ₑ The word came into English via French from Latin *cavillari* 'to scoff', from *cavilla* 'mockery'.

celsitude
noun
1 elevated position; high rank; eminence
2 exalted character
3 height; tallness

chapitle
noun
a chapter
ₑ This is an obsolete variant of 'chapter' which was used in reference to both book chapters and ecclesiastical chapters.

chare
noun
a narrow lane or alley
ₑ Many regions of Great Britain have charming dialect terms for alleys. 'Chare' is particularly common in north-east England – others include 'snicket' (northern England), 'twitten' (Sussex), 'wynd' (Scotland), and 'ginnel' (northern England and Scotland).

charientism
noun
an expression of a disagreeable thing in a pleasant manner, eg a gracefully veiled insult

charoset(h) or haroset(h)
noun
a rough paste made from a mixture of finely chopped nuts, fruit, spices, etc mixed with wine
   🍯 Charoset is eaten with bitter herbs at the Jewish Passover meal. The word is derived from a Hebrew word meaning 'potter's clay', and the paste symbolizes the clay from which the Israelites made bricks in Egypt.

chartophylax
noun
(in the Orthodox Christian churches) an ecclesiastical official with judicial responsibilities
   🍯 The term refers specifically to the officer responsible for the official records and documents of the Patriarch of Constantinople.

cheewink
noun
a long-tailed North American finch *Pipilo erythrophthalmus*
   🍯 This bird is also known as the towhee.

chiliasm
noun
(in Christian theology) the belief that there will be a golden age or paradise on Earth when Jesus will reign for 1,000 years prior to the final judgment; millenarianism
   🍯 The word is derived via Latin from Greek *chilias* 'thousand'. The word describing this belief is 'chiliastic'.

chino
noun
a strong cotton twill fabric, usually khaki-coloured
   🍯 The surprising origin of this word is the Latin American Spanish word *chino*, meaning 'toasted'.

circurate
verb
to tame, or reclaim from a wild state

claque
noun
1 a group of people hired to applaud a performer in a theatre etc, or a speaker at a meeting
2 a circle of admirers or flatterers

   ঠ➤ The concept of the claque has its origins in ancient Greek theatre, where poets and playwrights attempted to sway the decisions of competition judges by employing the services of a claque to show noisy appreciation of their works to the detriment of their opponents. The poet Philemon, one of the first 'celebrities', wildly popular with the Athenian public, was a successful proponent of this technique, frequently beating his intellectually superior, but less popular, opponent Menander in theatrical competitions. The English word is derived from French *claquer* 'to clap' and originates in 19th-century Paris where legions of influential *claqueurs*, *rieurs* (laughers) and *pleureuses* (weepers) worked together in practically every theatre.

cleek
noun
1 a large hook or crook used to catch hold of, pull or suspend something
2 a type of golf club
verb
to catch hold of, seize, clutch, grasp, or snatch

   ঠ➤ Common in northern English dialect from medieval times, the word now survives mainly in Scots.

clerisy
noun
educated and cultured people considered as a group; the intelligentsia

   ঠ➤ The word is derived from German *Klerisei*, meaning 'clergy', from Latin *clericus* 'priest'.

cleruch

noun

an Athenian who was granted land in another country but retained his Athenian citizenship

> A body of cleruchs, or the land allocated to them, was known as a 'cleruchy'.

clype

verb

to tell tales about; to inform against

> This is a Scots dialect word originating from Middle English *clepien* meaning 'to call'.

cockalorum

noun

1 a little or young cockerel

2 a bumptious little person

3 boastful talk; crowing

cocum

adjective

1 lucky, advantageous, providing opportunity

2 correct, proper

> The word is pronounced '*koh*-kum', rhyming with 'hokum'.

coff

verb

to buy, purchase

> This is a Scots dialect word derived from Middle Dutch *copen* 'to buy'.

cogware

noun

a coarse, heavy woollen cloth similar to frieze

coleta

noun

a pigtail or ponytail

ತಿ The word is applied especially to the pigtail worn by a bullfighter as a sign of his profession.

colombophile

noun

a pigeon-fancier

ತಿ This lovely-sounding word is derived from Latin *columba* 'dove' and Greek *philos* 'lover'.

comiconomenclaturist

noun

someone who collects or studies funny personal names

ತಿ Just as I have become interested in building up my collection of unusual and funny words, it would seem that there are plenty of people who pass their time drawing up lists of funny names, with seemingly endless examples to choose from. Some of these names are apparently real (Ima Hogg, Shanda Lear, Mrs Burns the baker, et al) but many are the inventively suggestive coinages so beloved by comics, cabaret acts, Bond girls and porn stars, most of which are too fruity for inclusion here.

commensal

noun

1 either of two different organisms living in a close association from which one species benefits and the other is unaffected
2 a person who eats at the same table as another; a dining companion or mess-mate

comploration

noun

lamentation (by a number of people united in grief)

compotation

noun

the act of drinking together; a drinking party

ತಿ The word is derived from Latin *com-* 'together' and *potare* 'to drink' and is a deliciously grand word for the joyful act of carousing in the company of one's fellow compotators.

concatenate
verb
to link a number of items together into a series, eg a chain of events

concupiscence
noun
strong desire, especially sexual desire

condign
adjective
well-deserved, fitting
> ટ The word is derived from Latin *condignus*, from *dignus* 'worthy', and is usually used of a punishment.

conepatl or conepate
noun
an American skunk
> ટ The name is derived from Native Mexican *cone-* 'young, little' and *epatl* 'fox'

confabulate
verb
1 to talk, chat or confer
2 to imagine experiences, usually as compensation for loss of memory
> ટ As the only male in a home which I share with a wife and three daughters, the first sense of the verb 'confabulate' is one which is familiar and dear to me. One of my favourite expressions, it aptly describes the pervading soundtrack to my home life – a happy and constant background noise of chatter. The word is derived from Latin *confabulari* 'to talk together', from *fabula* 'tale', which is also at the root of 'fable' and 'fabulous'.

confert
adjective
compressed, crowded, thick, dense

conflate
verb
to combine or blend two items into a single whole

ৎ The word is used particularly of the blending of two variant texts or differing stories. The noun formed from this verb is 'conflation'.

congeries
noun
a collection of articles randomly heaped up together
ৎ The word is derived from the Latin *congerere* 'to heap up'

congruous
adjective
suitable, fitting
ৎ The word is derived from Latin *congruere* which means 'to meet together'.

contango
noun
(on the Stock Exchange) a situation in futures trading where the price of a commodity for future delivery is higher than the price for immediate settlement, and the amount by which the two prices differ
ৎ Disappointingly unrelated to the Argentinian dance, this word instead derives arbitrarily from the word 'continue'. Historically, 'contango' was used of a situation where a buyer of stock wished to defer settlement and paid the seller a fee for this deferment.

contrectation
noun
1 handling, touching, especially sexual foreplay
2 an impulse, even compulsion, to caress someone of the opposite sex
ৎ In Roman law, the term was used of the removal and handling of someone's property against their wishes.

contrist
verb
to make sad, deject

contrude
verb
to push together, to crowd

contumacy

noun

stubborn refusal to obey or comply; resistance to authority

→ This handy word, which originates from Latin *contumax* 'insolent', is one which I find more and more useful as I get older. In common with many other 'grumpy old men', I find it increasingly difficult to be dictated to by the powers above, and am ever more tempted to wilfully disobey.

contumely

noun

1 scornful or insulting treatment

2 a contemptuous insult

3 disgrace

conulata

noun

a tentacled cone-shaped marine organism

→ This organism existed from the Cambrian to the Triassic periods, and is known from fossil remains.

copintank

noun

a 16th-century hat with a high crown in the shape of a sugar loaf

→ Other spellings of this word include 'copentank' and 'coptank'.

corkir

noun

1 a lichen formerly used in dyeing

2 the red or purple colour produced by the dye

→ The word is derived from Gaelic *corcur* meaning 'crimson'.

coruscate

verb

to sparkle, to give off flashes of light

coulee

noun

1 a lava-flow, either molten or solidified

2 (in western areas of Canada and the USA) a deep gulch or ravine, usually dry in summer

3 (in southern USA) a stream or dry stream-bed

coxcomb

noun

a vain or conceited man; a dandy

   ह॒ The word is a variant form of 'cockscomb' and originally meant 'a jester', in reference to the jester's traditional comb-like cap.

crapulous or crapulent

adjective

1 drunk; suffering from sickness caused by overdrinking

2 resulting from intemperance

3 tending to indulge in alcohol

   ह॒ A wonderfully onomatopoeic word which sums up so perfectly the feelings with which many of us are so familiar after a period of over-indulgence. The word is derived via Latin *crapula* meaning 'intoxication', from Greek *kraipale* 'drunken headache'. As such it is, perhaps surprisingly, unrelated to the origins of the word 'crap', which finds its origins in Middle English *crappe* 'chaff'.

craw-craw

noun

(in West Africa) an itchy skin disease that may result in ulceration

   ह॒ The name is derived from Dutch *kraauw* 'scratch', and the disease can afflict animals as well as humans.

crazia

noun

a copper coin used in Tuscany until the mid 19th century

   ह॒ This extravagant-sounding coin was worth about one-twelfth of a lira – an amount which in today's terms would be infinitessimal. At the time of the introduction of the euro as Italy's official currency in 2002, one lira was worth just under $1/3000$ of a pound, so a crazia would be worth around $^1/_{36000}$ of a pound, or $^1/_{360}$ of a penny. The word is pronounced '*krat*-si-uh'.

creance

noun
1 faith, belief, creed
2 (in falconry) the fine cord attached to a hawk's leash during its training to prevent it flying away

crepuscular

adjective
1 relating to twilight; dim
2 denoting animals that are active or appear at morning or evening twilight
  ∼ I find this evocative word, and its alternative 'crepusculous', to be vivid and descriptive of the magical period of twilight. 'Crepuscular' animals include cats, mice, deer and moose, and within this group are the 'matinal' (dawn) and enchantingly named 'vespertine' (dusk) groups.

Crichton

noun
a person who excels in all kinds of studies and pursuits
  ∼ The term is derived from the name of the 16th-century Scottish polymath and adventurer James Crichton of Cluny; in the 17th century his name became coupled with the epithet 'admirable'. The correct pronunciation is '*krai*-tun', rhyming with 'frighten'.

crinal

adjective
of or relating to the hair

crivens

exclamation
(Scots dialect) an expression of astonishment
  ∼ The word is sometimes preceded by 'by' or 'holy', and is possibly a corruption of 'Christ defend us'.

crockard

noun

a forged English penny

> ॐ This coin was produced in the Low Countries in the late 13th century and banned by Edward I in a statute of 1300.

croydon-sanguine

adjective

sallow-coloured

> ॐ The word is usually used of the complexion.

crump

noun

1 a loud, dull sound, such as the explosion of shell or bomb
2 a heavy blow

verb

1 to explode with a crumping sound
2 to crunch or crush something with the teeth
3 to make a crunching sound

cucumiform

adjective

like or having the shape or appearance of a cucumber

> ॐ The word is pronounced 'kyoo-*kyoo*-mi-fawm', with the stress on the second syllable.

Culdee

noun

a member of an ancient monastic order which had settlements in Ireland and Scotland from the 8th to the 14th century

> ॐ The name is derived from Irish *Céle Dé* 'God's comrade or ally', which was Latinized as *Coli dei*.

culicifuge

noun

a substance that is applied to the body or clothing to repel mosquitoes, gnats, etc

culorum

noun

a conclusion, or 'moral'

ᕂ The word occurs only in the writings of the medieval poet William Langland and is believed to be either a corruption of the final words of the Gloria in the Mass, or a derivation from Latin *corollarium* 'corollary'.

curmudgeon

noun

a bad-tempered, mean-spirited or miserly person

ᕂ This is a delightful word which so eloquently evokes an unpleasant or avaricious person. It is a word which I use often, but of course always with reference to others rather than myself!

currawong

noun

any of several varieties of Australian songbird of the genus *Strepera* resembling a magpie

ᕂ The name is derived from the Aboriginal word *garawan*.

cynosure

noun

1 the focus of attention, or centre of attraction or admiration

2 something that acts as a guide; a guiding star

ᕂ The word is derived from Greek *kynos* 'dog' and *oura* 'tail'; the name *kynosoura* ('the dog's tail') was given to the constellation Ursa Minor, which acted as a guide for sailors.

Dd

dactylogram
noun
a finger-print

dactylology
noun
the use of the hands and fingers to communicate, as in sign language

daedal
adjective
1 ingenious and complicated in design or function; intricate
2 showing or needing skill to make or use
> ৶ The word is derived from the name of Daedalus, the Athenian deviser
> and builder of the Labyrinth of Minos in Greek mythology.

daff
verb
1 to divest oneself of; to put off; to put aside
2 (in Scots dialect) to act or talk in either a foolish or a sportive
manner

daggett
noun
a tar obtained from the European white birch tree for use in tanning
and medicine

dander

noun

1 dandruff; scurf from the coat or feathers of various animals
2 anger, indignation; passion
3 (or dunder) the lees or dregs of sugarcane juice, used in the fermentation of rum
4 the vitrified refuse of a smith's fire or a furnace; a piece of slag

    The origins of the common phrase 'to get someone's dander up', meaning 'to make someone angry' are unclear. The phrase is first recorded in the early 19th century, and scholars are divided as to whether the 'dander' of the phrase is dandruff, or the frothing, seething ferment used to make rum.

dangleation

noun

dallying with girls, flirtation

    A pleasingly suggestive term which has sadly fallen into disuse in modern times, although the concept certainly remains very much alive. Flirtatious and womanizing men were known as 'danglers' and were particularly active at court and in high society. In an 18th-century letter, Henrietta Howard, Countess of Suffolk, writes to a lady friend bemoaning the dreariness of court life in the early years of the reign of George II: 'Hampton Court is very different from the place you knew ... Frizelation, flirtation and dangleation are now no more ...'

dapatical

adjective

sumptuous, lavish (in provision of food and drink)

    The word is derived from Latin *dapaticus*, from *daps* meaning 'feast'.

dasyphyllous

adjective

having hairy or downy leaves

    The word is derived from Greek *dasys* meaning 'hairy' and *phyllon* meaning 'leaf'. It is pronounced 'das-i-*fil*-us', with the stress on the third syllable.

dasypygal
adjective
having hairy buttocks
> ᖷᖇ The word is derived from Greek *dasys* meaning 'hairy' and *pyge* meaning 'buttocks'. It is pronounced 'das-i-*pai*-gul', with the stress on the third syllable.

dead man's fingers
noun
the common name or nickname of a fungus (*Xylaria polymorpha*), a coral (*Alcyonium digitatum*), and various orchids, because of their resemblance to a decomposing hand

deblaterate
verb
to prattle, blab, babble

decalcomania
noun
the process of transferring paint, pictures or designs from specially prepared paper onto another surface
> ᖷᖇ This technique was developed in the mid 1860s in Russia, and from there spread to America and Europe. It was used to great effect by surrealist artists in the early 1900s and is still popular today in the guise of 'blot paintings' so beloved of young children.

decanal
adjective
1 relating to a dean or deanery
2 relating to the south side of a choir in a church or cathedral
> ᖷᖇ The word is pronounced 'dek-*ay*-nul', with the stress on the second syllable. The second sense arose because the dean of a cathedral sits on the south side of the choir. The opposite term 'cantorial' relates to the north side of a cathedral, where the cantor, or singing leader, sits.

decatessarad
noun
a poem of 14 lines

declinograph
noun
an astronomical instrument for recording automatically the declination of stars

decollate
verb
1 to behead
2 to truncate

&> Sir John Gate, the first secular owner of my home, Beeleigh Abbey, after the Reformation, was beheaded on Tower Hill in 1553 for espousing the cause of Lady Jane Grey. Contemporary accounts record that the executioner had to use three strokes of the axe in order to achieve decollation. The ghost of Sir John is reputed to haunt the abbey, but I have yet to meet him.

decorticate
verb
to remove the outer layer from the bark, rind, husk, etc of a plant or fruit, or the surface layer, membrane, etc from an organ of the body

decrescent
adjective
decreasing; becoming gradually less; (of the Moon) waning

decury
noun
(in the army of ancient Rome) a squad of ten men commanded by a decurion

decus
noun
an old coin worth one crown

&> This slang name for the coin came about because it bore the Latin words 'decus et tutamen', a quotation from Virgil's *Aeneid*. The phrase, which means 'a glory and a safeguard', can also be found on modern British pound coins.

defalcation

noun

1 (in law) the misappropriation of property, especially money, held in trust; the amount misappropriated

2 the reduction of something by taking a part away, especially by cutting or lopping off

ও The word is derived from Latin terms *de-* 'away' and *falcare* 'to cut'.

defenestration

noun

the act of throwing someone or something out of a window

defterdar

noun

the official in charge of the financial affairs of a Turkish province

deglubate

verb

to excoriate; to flay

ও The literal meaning of this word is 'to remove the husk from'.

deglute

verb

to swallow

delatory

adjective

relating to an accusation or information laid against someone, especially in the case of punishable offences

delibate

verb

1 to sample by taking a sip or taste of

2 to dabble in

deliquesce

verb

1 to dissolve, melt

2 (in chemistry) to dissolve in water absorbed from the air

deliriant
noun
a poison that causes persistant delirium or mental aberration

delubrum
noun
1 an ancient Roman temple or shrine
2 a font, or a place of worship containing a font

delumbate
verb
to lame, maim or emasculate
    Ѧ The word is derived from Latin *delumbare* which means 'to make lame', and is generally used in a figurative sense.

demembration
noun
(in Scots law) dismemberment, mutilation, the cutting off of a limb

demersal
adjective
(of fish etc) existing on or close to the bottom of a sea or lake
    Ѧ Fish and other organisms that live on or near the surface of the sea are described as 'pelagic'.

demiurge
noun
1 (in some belief systems, especially Platonism and Gnosticism) a deity who created the physical universe and the physical aspect of humanity
2 a powerful creative force
    Ѧ The word is pronounced '*dem*-i-urj', with the stress on the first syllable. It is derived from the Greek *demiourgos*, meaning 'craftsman' or 'artisan'; in sense 1, the deity was usually seen as subordinate to a Supreme Being, and in some belief systems as the originator of evil. Such a being or force is described as 'demiurgic'.

demophil

noun

a friend of the people; someone fond of crowds or the masses

demot

noun

a member of an ancient Greek deme, one of the townships in the region around Athens

dennebol or danebol

noun

(in South Africa) a pine cone

dentil

noun

each of a series of rectangular or square blocks or projections set under the moulding of a cornice in classical architecture

ॐ The word is derived from an obsolete French word *dentille*, a diminutive of *dent* 'tooth', because such decorative features resemble a row of teeth.

dentiloquy

noun

the act or practice of speaking through clenched teeth

deontic or deontics

noun

(in philosophy) the study of duty and obligations as ethical concepts

ॐ The word is derived from Greek *deein* which means 'to be necessary or right'.

deracinate

verb

1 to tear up by the roots
2 to obliterate or eradicate something

dern or derne

noun
a private gate or door
adjective
1 hidden; concealed; secret
2 dark; dreary; desolate

▷ This is a Scots and northern English dialect word derived from the Old English *derne* 'to hide, conceal, keep secret'.

derobement

noun
(in fencing) evasion of the opponent's attempt to take or beat the blade while keeping the sword arm straight and threatening the opponent

derodidymus

adjective
having two heads

▷ The word is derived from the Greek terms *deire* meaning 'neck' and *didymus* meaning 'twin'. It is pronounced 'de-roh-*did*-i-mus', with the stress on the third syllable.

derringer

noun
a short large-bore pistol named after its American inventor, the gunsmith Henry Derringer

desipient

adjective
foolish, silly, enjoying trifles

desuetude

noun
1 a state of disuse
2 the discontinuance of a habitual practice

▷ The word is pronounced 'dis-*yoo*-it-yood', with the stress on the second syllable.

detumescence

noun

reduction, subsidence or lessening of swelling, especially the return of a swollen organ or other part of the body to its normal size

devanagari

noun

the script in which Sanskrit, Hindi and other Indian languages are usually written and printed

ࣷ The word is Sanskrit, meaning 'town-script of the gods'. It is pronounced 'day-vuh-*nah*-guh-ri', with the stress on the third syllable.

devel

noun

a severe and stunning blow

verb

to strike or beat

dextrad

adverb

towards the right side; dextrally

diamantigerous

adjective

yielding or producing diamonds

diaphanous

adjective

(of fabrics) light, fine and almost transparent

ࣷ The word comes from Greek *dia* 'through' and *phanein* 'to show'.

diaskeuast

noun

an editor or reviser, especially of old revisions of Greek texts

ࣷ The word is pronounced 'dai-uh-*skyoo*-ast', with the stress on the third syllable.

diaulos
noun
1 (in ancient Greece) a foot-race in which contestants turned at the end of the course and raced back to the starting point
2 (in architecture) a peristyle around a courtyard with two rows of columns, to prevent rain being driven into the inner part

dictitate
verb
to declare

didapper
noun
a small diving bird, such as a dabchick
 ⁁ The word is pronounced '*dai*-dap-uh', with the stress on the first syllable.

diddy
noun
1 a woman's breast or nipple
2 the teat of an animal
adjective
small, tiny

Digby (chick)
noun
a dried or smoked herring of a type caught off Digby in Nova Scotia, Canada

dilatancy
noun
dilation or expansion, especially the increase in volume of a granular substance when its shape is changed

dilly bag
noun
(Australian Aboriginal) a bag or basket made with plaited rushes or bark

diluvy
noun
a deluge
> ࣿ This word was in use in medieval times, generally referring to the Biblical flood survived by Noah and his family. The adjective 'diluvian' is still used nowadays, but 'diluvy' is much rarer.

dimane
verb
to flow, spring or originate from

dimaris
noun
(in logic) a term describing a type of four-part categorical syllogism

dimerous
adjective
1 (in entomology) having two joints, as in the tarsus of some insects
2 (in botany) having parts, such as petals, sepals, etc, in sets of two

dingus
noun
1 a gadget; a contraption
2 a person or thing whose name one cannot, or will not, remember.
> ࣿ A South African alternative for the same idea is 'dinges'. Like English 'thingummy', both are derived from *ding*, which means 'thing' in Afrikaans and Dutch.

diple
noun
(in grammar) a marginal mark used by ancient grammarians to indicate where an amendment is needed
> ࣿ The word is pronounced '*dip*-lee', with the stress on the first syllable.

dirhinous
adjective
having paired nostrils

diribitory
noun
a place where soldiers are mustered and receive their pay

discalceate or discalced
adjective
barefoot or wearing only sandals, especially of certain orders of friars and nuns

    ও The word is pronounced 'dis-*kal*-see-ayt', with the stress on the second syllable. It is derived from Latin *dis-* 'not' and *calceatus* 'shod', from *calceus* 'shoe'.

discombobulate
verb
(North American slang) to disconcert or discomfort someone

discursive
adjective
1 (in speech or writing) rambling, wandering from the point
2 (in philosophy) based on argument and reason (rather than intuition)

displat
verb
to untwist, unplait

disquisition
noun
a long and detailed discourse on a subject, in speech or writing

dissavage
verb
1 to tame
2 to civilize

dissave
verb
to live off savings or realized assets because one's income is inadequate

ళ The word was coined in the 20th century by economists; people who
live by these means are referred to by economists as 'dissavers'.

dissemble
verb
1 to conceal or disguise one's true feelings or intentions; act
hypocritically
2 to pretend or simulate feelings or intentions one does not have

dissight
noun
an eyesore; an unsightly or unpleasant object or prospect

dissimulate
verb
to conceal or disguise, especially one's feelings

distutor
verb
to be removed from the position of tutor

divagate
verb
to stray, wander, digress

docimasy
noun
1 (in ancient Greece) an inquiry into the character and background of
anyone aspiring to public office or to citizenship, especially of Athens
2 the practice or method of testing substances such as metallic ores,
drugs, etc, to ascertain their nature and quality

ళ The word is pronounced '*dos*-i-mus-i', with the stress on the first
syllable.

doigté
noun
(in fencing) fingering, or the use of the fingers and thumb to control
the weapon

dolmus
noun
(in Turkey) a taxi shared as a form of public transport

dolosity
noun
deceit; hidden spite

dontopedalogy
noun
the science of opening your mouth and putting your foot in it
  ❧ Prince Philip, Duke of Edinburgh, is credited with coining this word
    for his tendency to make faux pas.

dossil
noun
1 (in surgery) a small roll or plug of lint used to keep open a sore,
wound, etc
2 (in printing) a roll of cloth used to wipe off the face of a copper
printing plate while leaving the ink in the engraved lines
  ❧ The word is derived from Old English *dosil* meaning 'spigot', which
    ultimately stems from Latin *ducere* 'to lead, draw'.

doxastic
adjective
1 relating to or dependant on opinion; forming an opinion
2 (in epistemology) relating to a theory of knowledge in which a
belief is only held when there are other beliefs in that system to
support it

dringle
verb
to linger; to trickle; to expend time lazily or slowly

drogulus
noun
an entity, usually a disembodied being, whose presence cannot be
verified because it has no physical effects

ह➤ The word was coined in around 1957 by the British philosopher A J Ayer.

dropax
noun
a depilatory, traditionally made with pitch and oil

drossard or drossart
noun
a steward or high bailiff
ह➤ The word is derived from Old Teutonic, meaning 'one who presides at the meals of a company or retinue'.

drugget
noun
1 a coarse woven wool fabric
2 a protective covering for a table or floor made from this fabric
ह➤ The word is derived from French *droguet* meaning 'waste fabric',

drumly
adjective
turbid, clouded, troubled
ह➤ The word is found in Scots and northern English dialects.

dulcite
noun
melampyrin, a white sugar-like substance that can occur naturally in plants or be produced artificially
ह➤ This substance is also known as Madagascan manna because it occurs as an exudation in trees on the island.

dulia
noun
(in the Roman Catholic Church) the form of veneration given to saints and angels
ह➤ The word is derived via Latin from Greek *douleia* 'servitude'.

dumpoke

noun

a steamed dish of boned, stuffed meat, especially duck or chicken, with butter and herbs

ॐ Derived via Hindi from Persian *dam* 'breath' and *pukht* 'cooked', the word produces the most satisfying adjective: 'dumpoked'.

dunnock

noun

common name of the small European songbird *Prunella modularis*

ॐ The word is a diminutive of 'dun', meaning 'having a greyish-brown colour'. The bird is also called a hedge sparrow in Britain, though more correctly known as the hedge accentor.

duntle

verb

to knock; to dent with a blow

ॐ This dialect word is believed to be derived from Scots *dunt* 'to deal a heavy blow'.

dwile or dwyle

noun

a cloth used for household chores

ॐ The dialect term 'dwyle' for a cleaning cloth will be familiar to many readers in East Anglia, but those acquainted with the outdoor pub game known as dwyle flunking will almost certainly be fewer in number. The origins of this game are shrouded in mystery – some insist it has its roots firmly planted in ancient Suffolk harvest rituals, others link the game to the court of Richard III. Others, perhaps more plausibly, credit some slightly inebriated Suffolk printers with the invention of the game in the 1960s. Dwile flunking involves using a stick to hurl a rag soaked in stale beer at an opposing team, the person who is doused in this way becoming the next wielder of the stick. Annual dwyle flunking championships were held in Suffolk throughout the 1960s and 1970s, and although these are no more, to this day it is not unheard of to see dwyle flunkers outside Suffolk pubs on lazy summer evenings.

dyscalculia
noun
impairment of the ability to calculate, solve mathematical problems, etc; it can be congenital or the result of brain injury

dysgenesis
noun
1 an abnormal or defective development of organs or parts, especially the gonads
2 infertility between hybrids

dyslogy
noun
censure; dispraise; unfavourable speech
  ફ☙ The word is formed from Greek *dys-* 'bad, difficult' and *logos* 'discourse' by analogy with 'eulogy', of which it is the opposite, although the word did not exist in classical Greek.

dysprosody
noun
a disorder which impairs aspects of speech such as stress, rhythm and intonation
  ફ☙ The disorder is often found in sufferers from aphasia (qv).

dystopia
noun
1 a vision of human existence or society where conditions are nightmarish through deprivation or oppression
2 a work (usually literary) describing such a state
  ફ☙ The word is derived from Greek *dys-* 'bad, difficult' and *topos* 'place'.

dystrophy
noun
the inadequate supply of nutrients to a part of the body

Ee

ebrillade

noun

(in equestrianism) the checking of a horse with the bridle; a jerk of one rein, given when the horse refuses to turn

ebullition

noun

1 a sudden, unrestrained expression of emotion
2 the state or appearance of boiling

&ptext; The word is derived from Latin *ebullire* 'to bubble up'.

ecdysis

noun

the process of shedding skin or an exoskeleton so that growth can occur

&ptext; The process occurs in animals with a rigid exoskeleton, such as insects and crustaceans. It is pronounced '*ek*-dis-is', with the stress on the first syllable. 'Ecdysiast', a word derived from this, is a facetious term for a striptease performer.

ectene

noun

(in the Orthodox Christian churches) a litany recited by a deacon with responses by the choir or congregation

edaphic
adjective
1 (in botany) of or relating to the soil
2 (in ecology) influenced by the soil

effendi
noun
(in Turkey) the form of address in speech equivalent to 'Mr'

effulgent
adjective
shining brightly, radiant, brilliant

egede
adjective
foolish

egestive
adjective
relating to the process of eliminating or expelling from the body
    〠 The word is derived from Latin *e-* 'out of' and *gerere* 'to carry'. The body's egestive processes include perspiration, evacuation of the bowels, etc.

egregious
adjective
outstandingly bad, outrageous or shocking
    〠 The literal meaning of Latin *egregius* is 'standing out from the herd', from *e-* 'out of' and *grex* 'herd'.

eidetic
adjective
1 (of a mental image) unusually clear and vivid, as if actually visible
2 (of a person or memory) able to reproduce a vivid visual image of something seen previously
noun
a person with this ability

ꝫ The word is pronounced 'ai-*det*-ik', with the stress on the second syllable.

ekker
noun
(British public school and Oxbridge college slang) exercise

eldritch
adjective
1 weird, uncanny
2 hideous
ꝫ Originally a Scots word, this is also in use in North America.

electuary
noun
a medicinal paste made by mixing a drug with a syrup, honey or preserve so that it can be administered orally
ꝫ The word is derived, via Late Latin and Middle English, from the Greek for 'to lick up or lick out'.

elephantry
noun
troops mounted on elephants
ꝫ The use of elephants in ancient warfare is well documented, and is believed to have originated in the Indian subcontinent around 1000 BC. Perhaps the best-known use of elephantry was during the Second Punic War between Rome and Carthage, when Hannibal and his troops invaded Italy by crossing the Alps, using their small North African forest elephants for shock value, with initially devastating effect. It did not take long for the Romans to learn to exploit the war elephants' tendency to panic, however, and thus render them obsolete. Other animals to have served in wars include troop-carrying camels, messenger dogs and mine-clearing giant rats.

elusion
noun
the act of evading, especially through adroitness or cunning

eluviation
noun
the lateral or downward movement of material in solution or suspension through soil

eluxate
verb
to displace, dislocate

emanationist
adjective
1 (in sociology) relating to the theory that behaviour is conditioned entirely by environment
2 (in theology) relating to the belief that the world was created by the emanation of spiritual beings

embat
noun
1 a northerly wind that blows across Egypt from Turkey
2 a local wind in Majorca
  ঌ 'Embat' is one of the many evocative names of local winds which I have come across during the compilation of this collection. Apart from the better-known winds such as the 'scirocco' and the 'mistral', other captivating winds include the snow-melting 'chinook', the dry, dusty 'harmattan', the boisterous 'levanter' and the sandstorm-producing 'habob'.

emblic
noun
the fruit of the *Emblica officinalis*, or Indian gooseberry

empyrean
noun
1 the highest heaven; the sphere of fire to the ancient world and the abode of God in the Christian tradition
2 (poetic) the sky
  ঌ The word is derived from Greek *empyros* 'fiery', and is pronounced 'em-*pi*-ri-un', rhyming with 'Syrian'.

emunctory

noun
any organ or passage of the body that discharges waste
adjective
conveying waste; relating to nose-blowing

enantiodromia

noun
a process by which a strong force produces its opposite, and the
interaction between the two

> ੴ The word is derived from Greek, meaning 'running in contrary ways'
> and was coined by the psychiatrist Carl Jung. It is usually applied to an
> individual's or society's adoption of beliefs opposite to those previously
> held. It is pronounced 'en-an-ti-oh-*droh*-mi-uh', with the stress on the
> fifth syllable.

enchiridion

noun
a handbook, manual; a concise source of information about a specific
subject or place

encomium

noun
a formal or high-flown expression of praise, in speech or writing

encopresis

noun
a medical term for defecation that is involuntary but not caused by a
physical defect or illness

endamask

verb
to paint or tinge a surface with various colours or shades of a colour,
producing the variation in pattern or shade characteristic of
damask

endemism
noun
the quality of being prevalent in or peculiar to a specific locality, region or people

endogamy
noun
1 (in anthropology) the practice of marrying only within the same group, eg a clan or tribe
2 (in botany) fertilization by pollen from another flower of the same plant

enfundying
verb
to be chilled; to become stiff or numb with cold

engastrimyth or engastrimuth
noun
a ventriloquist

engist
verb
to appoint the resting-places in (a journey)
   இ This old word was derived from Old French *en-* 'in' and *giste* (modern French *gîte*) 'resting- or stopping-place'. It was probably pronounced 'en-*jist*', with the stress on the second syllable.

entropy
noun
1 (in physics) the measure of the amount of disorder in a system
2 a measure of the unavailability of a system's energy for conversion into mechanical work

enuresis
noun
(in medicine) involuntary urination, especially while asleep

ephectic
adjective
suspending judgement; sceptical

epical
adjective
of or like a literary epic; grand, heroic

epicene
adjective
1 having characteristics of both sexes, or having no characteristics of either sex
2 relating to, or for use by, both sexes
3 effete

> ₰ In grammar, an epicene noun is one that applies to people or animals of either sex. It derives from Latin *epicoenus* 'of both genders', from Greek *epikoinos* 'common to many'.

epigastric
adjective
relating to the epigastrium, the part of the abdomen lying immediately over the stomach

epilogation
noun
a brief summing-up by way of conclusion

epiphragm
noun
a temporary plug of mucus which some molluscs use to close up the opening of their shell during a period of hibernation or aestivation

epiphyte
noun
(in botany) a plant that grows on another plant for support but is not a parasite, eg moss on a tree trunk

epistasis

noun

an interaction between genes, especially an interaction in which one gene modifies or suppresses the effect of another unrelated gene

epistemology

noun

(in philosophy) the theory of knowledge, especially its methods and validation

epitaxy

noun

(in crystallography) the growth of a crystal layer of one mineral on the crystal base of another mineral so that the crystal layers of both minerals have the same structural orientation

eponym

noun

1 the name of a person, place, etc after which something is named, especially a character in a play, novel, etc whose name provides the title

2 a name, title, etc derived from the name of a person, place, etc

> ट्ञ The word is derived from Greek *epi-* 'in addition' and *onyma* 'name'. The person who gives their name to something is described as 'eponymous'.

erotesis

noun

(in rhetoric) a figure of speech in which a question is asked that invites a strong assertion of the opposite

eructate

verb

to belch

eschatology

noun

1 the branch of theology dealing with death and final things, eg divine judgement, life after death

2 beliefs about the destiny of humankind and the world

    క్ష The word is derived from Greek *eschatos* 'last' and *logos* 'study'. It is pronounced 'es-kuh-*tol*-uh-ji', with the stress on the third syllable.

escheat

noun
1 the reversion of property to the state or (in feudal times) to a lord after its owner died without legal heirs
2 property reverting in this way
verb
1 to hand over property in this way
2 to confiscate

    క్ష The word is pronounced 'is-*cheet*', with the stress on the second syllable.

escrivan

noun
a clerk who sails on board a ship; a supercargo

esculent

noun
any edible substance
adjective
fit to eat; edible

ethereous

adjective
1 of or resembling ether
2 ethereal

etiolated

adjective
1 (of a plant) having yellow foliage through the exclusion of light
2 (of a person) having a wan and weak appearance

eudemonic or eudaemonic

adjective
producing or conducive to happiness and wellbeing

ॐ The word is derived from Greek *eudaimonismos* meaning 'system of happiness'.

eunuchry
noun
the state of being a eunuch

eupeptic
adjective
having good digestion

euphonious or euphonic
adjective
sounding pleasant, harmonious

euphuist
noun
someone who affects an excessively elegant or high-flown style of speaking or writing
ॐ The affected and bombastic literary style known as 'Euphuism' was brought briefly into vogue in British literature by John Lyly's romance *Euphues: The Anatomy of Wit*, published in 1579. The concept takes its name from the Greek term *euphyes* meaning 'graceful or goodly'.

euroclydon
noun
a tempestuous north-east wind in the Mediterranean

eval
adjective
of or relating to an age or the duration of a period of time

evanescent
adjective
1 fading quickly
2 transitory, fleeting

exauctorate
verb
to deprive of authority or office; to oust; to discharge

excarnation
noun
the act of depriving or divesting of flesh
> ৼ In archaeology and anthropology this term is used of the burial practices of societies that remove the flesh of the dead and leave only the bones, such as the Tibetan sky burial.

excipulum
noun
the outer layer of cells partially enclosing the fructification of most lichens

excoriate
verb
1 to strip, peel or abrade skin from a person or animal
2 to criticize severely

exegesis
noun
1 a critical explanation of a text
2 the branch of theology concerned with the interpretation of the Bible

exercitor
noun
(in Roman law) a person with the right to receive a ship's earnings

exheredate
verb
to disinherit

exiguous
adjective
scanty, meagre; insufficient

eximious

adjective

select; excellent

    ࣸ This is a beautiful-sounding word which is sadly all but lost to modern English. It lives on, however, in the name of a suitably magnificent London boutique.

exodontia

noun

exodontics; the branch of dentistry dealing with the extraction of teeth

exogenous

adjective

originating from or growing outside something

exorability

noun

the condition or capability to be moved by entreaties; tender-heartedness

exordium

noun

the introductory section of a discourse or speech

    ࣸ The word is derived from Latin *exordiri* 'to begin'.

expatiate

verb

to speak or write at length and in detail; to elaborate

    ࣸ The word is derived from Latin *expatiari* meaning 'to digress'.

expergefactor

noun

someone or something that awakens a sleeper, eg an alarm clock

expilation

noun

1 the act of spoliation; pillage; plunder

2 (in civil law) the crime of abstracting the goods of the deceased before the heir has taken possession of them

expiscate
verb
to search out; to find out by skilful or persistent investigation
> ৡ This word is derived from Latin *ex-* 'out' and *piscari* 'to fish'. Such a process is described as 'expiscatory'.

expugnation
verb
the process of taking by storm, overcoming in a fight, vanquishing
> ৡ This word is derived from Latin *ex-* 'out' and *pugnare* 'to fight'.

exsanguinate
verb
to drain or deprive of blood

exsibilate
verb
to hiss off the stage; to reject with a hissing sound

exspuition
noun
the act of discharging saliva by spitting

exungulate
verb
to trim or cut (nails, hoof, etc)

fabiform
adjective
shaped like a bean

facinorous
adjective
extremely wicked
> ༀ The word is pronounced 'fa-*sin*-uh-rus', with the stress on the second syllable.

factitious
adjective
artificial or contrived, rather than genuine or natural

fady
adjective
tending to fade; fading gradually to a paler hue

faggot vote
noun
(19th-century British political slang) the practice of increasing votes for party purposes by partitioning residential property into a number of apartments so that more residents were eligible to vote

fainhead
noun
gladness; willingness

falderal or folderol
noun
1 a meaningless refrain in a song
2 a piece of nonsense or flippancy
3 a toy; a trifling object, a bauble

famelic
adjective
1 relating to hunger; hungry; starving
2 exciting hunger; mouth-watering

famulate
verb
to serve

famulus
noun
a close attendant, such as a private secretary

fandangle
noun
1 an extravagantly fanciful ornament
2 tomfoolery, nonsense

fanglomerate
noun
(in geology) a conglomerate (rock consisting of a variety of stones
that have been fused together) formed deep within an alluvial fan,
usually in desert environments

fank
noun
a sheep-fold; a walled or fenced pen for sheep

verb

to pen up

> ٷ The word is derived from the unlikely-sounding Gaelic word for a sheep-pen: *fang*.

farol

noun

(in bullfighting) a two-handed movement in which the bullfighter passes the cape over his own head

farouche

adjective

1 shy

2 sullen

3 socially inexperienced

> ٷ This comes from the Old French meaning 'wild' and 'shy', and comes ultimately from the Latin *foras* 'out of doors'.

farraginous

adjective

varied; miscellaneous; indiscriminate; a hotch-potch

> ٷ The word is derived from Latin *farrago* 'mixed fodder for cattle' (hence, figuratively, 'a confused mixture').

farse

noun

an amplification or comment in the vernacular language, on part of a church service or Bible passage in Latin

verb

to extend by interpolation

> ٷ It was a common practice to include these commentaries in religious texts before the Reformation led to the translation of the Bible and the use of the vernacular language for church services in Protestant countries. Interestingly, the term is directly derived from the word 'farce', presumably due to its links with interpolation – inserting a word or passage into a book or manuscript – presumably in this case without the intention to mislead, however.

fasciole
noun
one of a band of minute tubercles, bearing modified spines, on the shells of spatangoid sea urchins

Fastingong
noun
Shrove Tuesday, ie the day before the beginning of the Christian season of Lent
> ॐ Despite its exotic sound, this word is in fact derived from Middle English *faste* 'fast' and *ingong* 'beginning'.

fastuous
adjective
1 proud, haughty, disdainful
2 pretentious, ostentatious, showy

fatidical or fatidic
adjective
having the ability to foretell future events; prophetic
> ॐ The word is derived from Latin *fatum* 'prophecy, doom' and *dicere* 'to say'.

feak
noun
a curling lock of hair, especially one that is dangling

feauges
noun
a disease that affected colonists of the Bermudas in the early 17th century; the main symptom was extreme weakness through lack of food

febrifuge
noun
a medicine or treatment that reduces fever
> ॐ The word is derived from *febrifugia*, the Latin name for the herb feverfew, which has been used since ancient times in medical preparations to relieve pain and inflammation.

feculent

adjective

1 polluted; fetid, filthy

2 containing sediment or faeces

    ?? The word is derived from Latin *faeculentus* meaning 'full of dregs'.

feis

noun

an Irish or Scottish festival of the arts similar to the Welsh Eisteddfod

    ?? The word is derived from Irish *feis* 'meeting, assembly'. In earlier times, it was an assembly of the kings, chieftains, priests, bards, etc of Ireland for legislative, social or literary purposes.

felicide

noun

the killing of a cat

feme

noun

(in law) a wife

    ?? In this context, man and wife are described as 'baron and feme'.

feminivorous

adjective

feeding on the flesh of women

fenage

noun

a hay crop

    ?? The word is derived from Latin *faenum*, meaning 'hay', via Old French *fener* 'to make hay'.

ferular or ferule

noun

a instrument, usually a flat ruler with a widened end, that was used for punishing children by beating them on the palms of their hands

    ?? A recipient of corporal punishment as a schoolboy, I find this word and the concept behind it extremely unpleasant. The etymology of 'ferule' is illuminating – the word is apparently derived from Latin *ferula* 'fennel stalk', as these were used in Roman times as instruments of punishment.

fetial

adjective

heraldic; ambassadorial; relating to the declaration of war or conclusion of peace treaties

    {} The word is derived from Latin *fetiales*, the name of a college of priests in ancient Rome involved with the religious ceremonies surrounding declarations of war and peace and who acted as heralds.

fetterlock

noun

1 a variant of 'fetlock'

2 a device for hobbling a horse

    {} A representation of a fetterlock was sometimes included on a coat of arms; it is believed that it signified that a knight had been taken prisoner or had ransomed another knight.

fidate

verb

to give immunity from capture

    {} The word is pronounced '*fai*-dayt', with the stress on the first syllable. It is usually used in reference to chess pieces.

filibeg

noun

a kilt

    {} The word is from Gaelic *feileadh* 'pleat or fold' and *beag* 'little'. It is sometimes spelt 'philabeg'.

fillister

noun

1 a rabbet on the outer edge of a sash window's bar which holds the putty and glass

2 a plane for making a rabbet

fissiparous
adjective
1 reproducing by fission
2 having a tendency to split
> ﹗ The word is derived from Latin *fissus* 'split' and *parere* 'to bring forth'. The noun is 'fissiparousness'.

fistic
adjective
relating to the fists, especially their use in boxing; pugilistic

fitchew
noun
the pole-cat, or its fur

flabellation
noun
the act of fanning, particularly in the context of keeping fractured limbs cool

flagitious
adjective
1 deeply criminal; utterly wicked
2 infamous; scandalous; shamefully disgraceful
> ﹗ The word is pronounced 'fluh-*jish*-us', rhyming with 'vicious'.

flapdoodle
noun
1 nonsense; foolish talk
2 a showy object of little value
> ﹗ A pleasing and evocative sounding word which sums up perfectly the empty talk and jibberish with which one is sometimes bombarded.

flap-dragon
noun
1 a game in which players caught raisins floating in flaming brandy and swallowed the raisins whole
2 the raisins used in this game

ও *Chambers Book of Days* of 1869 describes the peculiarly English game of 'flap-dragon' (or 'snapdragon') as a favourite sport for Christmas Eve. Handed down 'from time immemorial', it suggests that '... in this amusement we retain a trace of the fiery ordeal of the middle ages, and also of the Druidical fire-worship of a still remoter epoch'. No comment is made on the dubious merits of playing such a game in a time before proper healthcare and a regular fire service. The 'poor relation' of the game, popular among the 'common people', does attract some criticism however. Entailing the drinking of a can of ale or cider containing a burning candle, it is described as rather arduous and likely to cause singeing of the long beards and whiskers which were fashionable at the time.

fledgy

adjective
1 (of birds) feathered, feathery; fledged
2 (of young bees) ready to fly

flemensfirth

noun
the entertainment of fugitives

ও This is an Old English law term but the exact nature of the offence is unclear. It probably referred to the king's right to exact a penalty from anyone who had succoured a banished person.

flocculent

adjective
resembling or consisting of tufts of wool; woolly, fleecy, downy

flubdub

noun
(in the USA) bombastic or pretentious talk; nonsense

fogle

noun
(slang) a silk handkerchief

ও 'Fogle-hunter' was a slang term for a pickpocket.

fopdoodle
noun
a fool; a simpleton

forfex
noun
a pair of scissors or shears

formication
noun
the sensation, usually hallucinatory, that insects or snakes are
crawling over the skin

formosity
noun
beauty; comeliness

fougasse
noun
a mine buried in the ground so that its detonation buries enemy
troops by throwing debris over their position

francolin
noun
a partridge of the genus *Francolinus*, native to Africa and south Asia

frendent
adjective
gnashing the teeth

friagem
noun
a period of cold weather in the Amazon basin in Brazil and in eastern
Bolivia, caused by currents of cold air from Antarctica

fricative
adjective
(of a sound) made by the friction of breath through a narrowed opening

noun

a consonant whose sound is produced in this way, eg 'f', 'sh', 'th'

ह्ल The word is derived from Latin *fricare* meaning 'to rub'.

frigger

noun

a small glass ornament made by a craftsman in his own time

ह्ल The objects were usually made from the molten glass remaining in the pot at the end of the working day. They had no utilitarian purpose, taking whatever form satisfied the whim of the glass-maker.

frippet

noun

a frivolous or flighty young woman, who is inclined to show off

friscajoly

adjective

a refrain in jovial songs that has no meaning

ह्ल I take great pleasure from the playful sounds of the nonsensical words used to provide jovial refrains in early songs. 'Friscajoly' derives from the delightful 'frisco' listed below – the earliest citation in the *Oxford English Dictionary* dates from 1519 and reads 'Synge fryska joly, with hey troly loly'.

frisco

noun

a brisk leap or other movement made while dancing

frow or froe

noun

a cleaving tool with a wedge-shaped blade set at right angles to the handle

frubish

verb

to polish up; to burnish; to furbish

fucoid
noun
1 a member of the order Fucales, which includes brown algae
2 a fossilized cast or impression of a fucoid algae

fugleman
noun
1 a leader, especially a political leader, organizer or spokesman
2 (historically) a soldier who stood in front of a body of drilling soldiers as a model for the movements and time
→ The word is derived from German *Flügelmann* meaning 'file leader'.

fullend
verb
to end fully; to complete

fulsome
adjective
excessive to the point of being distasteful, cloying
→ This word should properly carry a pejorative sense, but it is often misapplied.

funambulist
noun
someone who walks or performs on ropes, eg a tightrope-walker
→ This seems at first sight to be a very apt word to describe the dangerous but entertaining sports of the tightrope-walker, although I was rather disappointed to learn that the 'fun' part of the word is actually derived from Latin *funis* meaning 'rope'.

fundament
noun
(jocular) the buttocks

furfuraceous
adjective
resembling bran or dandruff; scaly; scurfy
→ The word is derived from Latin *furfur* 'bran'.

furphy

noun

a false report or improbable story; a rumour

> ࿖ This Australian term originated in the early 20th century as a brand name of a water-cart – a precursor of the modern water cooler – around which improbable stories, rumours and gossip are still exchanged to this day.

fust

noun

1 (in architecture) the shaft of a column or trunk of a pilaster
2 a strong musty smell; mustiness

verb

1 to become mouldy
2 to smell musty

futilitarian

noun

relating to the view that all human endeavour is futile

futtock

noun

one of the curved timbers that forms a rib in a wooden ship's frame

fylfot

noun

a swastika

> ࿖ The word is pronounced '*fil*-fot', with the stress on the first syllable. Since World War II, the term 'swastika' has usually been reserved for the Nazi device, and 'fylfot' is used to describe the swastika (now with truncated arms) in heraldry and the similar device that appears in medieval stained-glass windows.

Gg

gabion
noun
1 a cylindrical wicker basket filled with earth and stones, formerly used in building fortifications etc
2 (in civil engineering) a hollow metal-mesh cage, usually filled with stones, which is used to build retaining walls, protect banks against erosion etc

galactophagous
adjective
feeding on milk
    ➤ The word is derived from Greek *gala* 'milk' and *phagein* 'to eat'.

galah
noun
1 an Australian cockatoo with a grey back and pink breast
2 (Australian slang) a fool, idiot

galeate
adjective
1 shaped like a helmet
2 (in zoology) having a galea, a helmet-shaped covering

galimatias
noun
confused, meaningless talk; gibberish

galliard
noun

a lively dance in triple time for couples, popular in the 16th and 17th centuries

→ The word is derived from French *gaillard* 'valiant'.

gallimaufry
noun

a jumble, a hodge-podge, a ridiculous medley

→ The word is derived from Old French *galimafrée*, a dish made by hashing up odds and ends of food.

gallivant
verb

to go about looking for entertainment or amusement

galoot
noun

(slang, especially USA) a clumsy person

→ This was originally a nautical slang term for a soldier or inexperienced sailor – someone who was unsteady on their feet at sea.

gamin (*masculine*) or gamine (*feminine*)
noun

1 a street urchin

2 an impudent child

3 (of a girl) someone with mischievous or boyish charm

gamp
noun

(colloquialism) an umbrella

→ This word is taken from the character of Mrs Gamp in Charles Dickens' novel *Martin Chuzzlewit*, who carried a large, unwieldy umbrella.

ganch
noun

1 a material with a high level of gypsum used in central Asia from the

10th century for brickmaking and for relief carvings

2 (in Northern Ireland) an ill-mannered person; an opinionated person, a loudmouth

verb

to drop from a height onto sharp stakes or hooks, a form of execution used by the Turks in medieval times

gansel

noun

a garlic sauce, served especially with goose

gastrula

noun

a stage of development in embryos of most species during which the three germ layers are formed from which the organs will develop

gavage

noun

the forced feeding of animals, usually by means of a tube passed into the stomach.

❧ The word is derived from French *gaver* 'to force down the throat'. The method is used to fatten up livestock for market, for example in the production of foie gras and veal, and to adminster medicines to sick animals.

gavial

noun

a large Indian crocodile with a long narrow snout, considered sacred by Hindus

❧ The word is a corruption of the Hindustani *ghariyal*, and is often spelt 'gharial'.

gaw

noun

a channel or furrow made with a spade or plough on the surface of soil to drain off water from a field, pond, etc

gemellion

noun

1 one of a pair of basins used for washing the hands before meals or as part of a church service

2 any decorative basin

    ॐ This word is derived from Latin *gemellus* meaning 'twin'.

geophagy

noun

the practice of eating earth or earthy substances such as chalk or clay

    ॐ The word is pronounced 'jee-*of*-uh-ji', with the stress on the second syllable, and is derived from Greek *ge* 'earth' and *phagein* 'to eat'.

gibbous

adjective

1 (of the Moon or a planet) more than half illuminated but not fully illuminated

2 swollen, protuberant

3 humped or humpbacked

    ॐ The word is derived from Latin *gibbus* meaning 'hump'.

giddea or gidya

noun

1 a species of Acacia tree

2 a long throwing spear made from the wood of the giddea tree, used by Australian Aborigines

gigantomachy

noun

a war of giants, especially the great battle in Greek mythology between the Gigantes (the race of giants born of Gaia, the primordal mother) and the Olympian gods

    ॐ The word is pronounced 'jai-gan-*tom*-uh-ki', with the stress on the third syllable.

giggit

verb

(in USA) to move rapidly, usually in some form of conveyance

gill-flirt or jill-flirt
noun
a thoughtless, giddy or wanton young woman

glebous
adjective
1 relating to a glebe, a piece of land that was part of a clergyman's benefice and provided him with income
2 earthy; cloddy; fertile
   ❧ The word is derived from Latin *glaeba* meaning 'clod, soil'.

gledge
noun
a sidelong glance; a quick look
verb
to give a sidelong glance; to squint

gleek
noun
1 a jest, trick or deception
2 an enticing glance
3 a game of cards for three players, popular in Britain in the 16th and 17th centuries
verb
1 to scoff, make sport, gibe
2 to fritter time
3 (slang) to squirt liquid (including saliva) through the teeth or from under the tongue

globose
adjective
having the shape of a sphere or ball; globular

glyconic
noun
a form of verse that consists of either three or four feet
   ❧ This form of verse is found in Greek and Latin poetry and is named after the Greek lyric poet Glycon.

gnathonical or gnathonic
adjective
sycophantic; fawning
› The word is derived from Gnatho, a parasite in Terence's play *Eunuchus*.

gnomic
adjective
1 relating to or consisting of maxims and aphorisms (gnomes)
2 moralizing
› The word is derived from Greek *gnomikos*, from *gnome* 'opinion'.

goddard
noun
a goblet

godivoe
noun
1 a type of forcemeat, usually including veal, chicken or fish
2 a pie made from this forcemeat

godown
noun
(in south-east Asia) a warehouse or storeroom
› This word is derived via Portuguese from Malay *godong*, which may come from a Telagu word meaning 'place where goods lie'. It is pronounced 'goh-*down*', with the stress on the second syllable.

gompa
noun
a Buddhist temple or monastery in Tibet

goniometry
noun
the measurement of angles; trigonometry

googol
noun
the number ten raised to the power of 100

ᏹ The word originated in the 1940s, and was reportedly the response of Milton Sirotta, the nine-year-old nephew of US mathematician Edward Kasner, when his uncle asked him to name the largest number he could imagine.

gormandizer
noun
1 someone who eats greedily and excessively; a guzzler
2 someone who indulges in good eating

gossoon
noun
a lad; a young male servant
ᏹ The word is derived from French *garçon* 'boy'.

gracile
adjective
slender; willowy

grallatorial
adjective
relating to long-legged wading birds, from the name of the order Grallatores
ᏹ The word is derived from Latin *grallator* 'stilt-walker', from *grallae* 'stilts'.

grame
noun
anger; passion; sorrow; distress; malice

graminivorous
adjective
(of animals) feeding on grass or cereals

graper
noun
the part of a lance by which it is grasped

grapholagnia
noun
a fascination with and urge to stare at sexually explicit and obscene pictures

gravigrade
adjective
moving with slow, heavy paces

greegree
noun
a West African charm, fetish or amulet

gremial
noun
1 a cloth laid across a bishop's knees when he sits during a Mass or ordination service
2 a bosom friend
adjective
relating to the lap or bosom

    ఈ The word is derived from Latin *gremium* 'lap'.

grenetine
noun
a type of gelatine obtained from young animals

gressorial
adjective
(in zoology) adapted for walking or stepping; having limbs adapted for walking; having the habit of walking

gride
verb
to cut, scrape or pierce, with a grating noise or so as to inflict intense pain

grimoire
noun
a book of magic written between the late Middle Ages and the 18th century

ᘒ An appropriately dark and forbidding-sounding word for books of spells and magic, which is in reality derived via French *gramaire* from the same root as 'grammar'. It was applied in the Middle Ages to books on Latin syntax and hence acquired the meaning of 'a book of instruction'.

grimpen
noun
(possibly) a marshy area

ᘒ Grimpen Mire is mentioned in the Sherlock Holmes story *The Hound of the Baskervilles* but it is not clear whether Conan Doyle invented the word or it already existed.

grinagog
noun
someone who is always grinning, especially foolishly and without reason

grith
noun
(in Old English law) protection, sanctuary or safe conduct guaranteed in certain circumstances, eg when in church; subsequently, a place of protection, a sanctuary, an asylum

groak
verb
to look or stare at longingly, especially at someone who is eating

ᘒ A very uncommon old word which I was unable to find in any dictionary. This is an ancient art still widely and ably practised by pet dogs everywhere.

groise
noun
(British public school slang) a swot or someone who curries favour

gromatics
noun
the art and practice of land-surveying

ᐅ The word is derived from Latin *gromatici*, the name of the professional class of land-surveyors in ancient Rome. They were named after the *groma* (or *gruma*) 'a surveyor's measuring rod'.

groyne
noun
a timber barrier or low, broad wall built out from a beach to break the force of the waves and so check erosion
ᐅ The word is derived via French from Latin *grunium* 'pig's snout'.

grume
noun
a thick viscous or clotted liquid, especially blood

guttle
verb
to eat greedily; to gorge

gynarchy
noun
a system of government in which the ruler is a woman or women
ᐅ The word is pronounced '*gai*-nah-ki', with the stress on the first syllable.

gyrovague
noun
a wandering monk of the Middle Ages
ᐅ This word is derived from Latin *gyrus* 'circuit' and *vagus* 'wandering'.

Hh

hagiography

noun

1 the writing of stories of saints' lives
2 a biography that idealizes its subject

&ctext; The word is derived from Greek *hagios* 'holy' and *graphe* 'writing'.

halalcor or halalkhor

noun

a member of one of the lowliest and most despised 'untouchable' groups in India etc, because as 'scavengers' they touch the dead

&ctext; The literal meaning is 'people to whom everything is lawful food'. The word is derived from Arabic *halal* 'a thing religiously lawful' and Persian *khur-dan* 'to eat'.

halcyon

adjective

1 calm; peaceful; tranquil
2 (of a period of time) prosperous, happy

noun

a bird of the genus *Halcyon*; a kingfisher

&ctext; This evocative word is derived from a mythical bird, identified with the kingfisher, that was believed to nest on the sea at the winter solstice and to have the power to calm the wind and waves.

halidom
noun
1 something considered holy or sacred
2 a holy place, a sanctuary

halieutics
noun
a treatise on fish or fishing

halitus
noun
breath; an exhalation

hamartia
noun
tragic flaw; the character flaw or error from which the downfall of a tragic hero ensues

Hamite
noun
1 a member of one of the groups of peoples of northern and north-eastern Africa (eg ancient Egyptians, Berbers, Tuaregs, etc), so-called because they were believed to be descended from Ham, one of the sons of Noah
2 the languages of these peoples

hammal
noun
(in Muslim countries in the Middle East) a porter

handsel
noun
a good-luck present given at the start of a new year, new undertaking, etc
verb
1 to give a handsel to someone
2 to inaugurate someone

੪ The word comes from Old English *handselen* 'giving into someone's hands' and Old Norse *handsal* 'giving of the hand in promise'. 'Handsel Monday' was an important holiday celebrated in Scotland and northern England on the first Monday of each new year. Small presents were exchanged and labourers enjoyed a welcome break from work, passing the day feasting and visiting friends.

haptodysphoria
noun
an unpleasant sensation felt by some people in response to certain tactile sensations

੪ Although I have no personal experience of this, it would seem to be a much more widespread affliction than I had at first imagined. During the compilation of this collection I have come across haptodysphorics who experience extreme reactions to anything from kiwi fruit and jelly to hamsters and old forks.

haptotropism
noun
(in botany) the tendency of certain plants to respond to touch by growing towards or wrapping tendrils around what is touching them

hardock or hordock
noun
a plant mentioned by Shakespeare that is tentatively identified with burdock

harmans
noun
(in old thieves' cant) the stocks

harpuisbos
noun
a shrub of the genus *Europs*, especially the resin bush, mostly found in southern Africa

੪ This Afrikaans word is approximately pronounced 'hah-puh-*ooz*-bos', with the stress on the third syllable.

harridan
noun
a bad-tempered old woman; a scold or nag
→ The origin is unclear but the word probably comes from French *haridelle* 'broken-down old horse'.

haver
verb
1 to talk nonsense; to babble
2 to vacillate, hesitate over a decision

havers
noun
(in Scots dialect) foolish talk, nonsense

haybote
noun
(in feudal times) a tenant's right to take timber from his landlord's estate to repair his hedges and fences
→ 'Bote' comes from Old English *bot* 'expiation, compensation, remedy'. The word was usually prefixed by another word that related to the goods that were to be repaired by the timber, as in 'house-bote' or 'plough-bote'. As 'hay' is an archaic term for 'hedge', 'haybote' was also known as 'hedgebote'.

hayward
noun
a hedge-warden
→ The hayward of a medieval manor or village was, like Little Boy Blue of the nursery rhyme, responsible for maintaining hedges and fences and ensuring that animals grazing on common land did not break into enclosed fields. The symbol of the hayward's office was a horn, which he would blow to warn of escaped cattle. Modern English has lost a wealth of words relating to the rural occupations, customs and traditions of our pre-industrial age, although 'hayward' is preserved as a fairly common surname.

hebberman
noun
someone who made a living fishing on the River Thames, usually downriver of London Bridge and on the ebbing tide

hebetate
verb
to make or become blunt or dull
adjective
blunt, with a soft point; dull

hecatontarchy
noun
government by 100 people

heckelphone
noun
a musical instrument of the oboe family, with a low pitch ranging between that of the bassoon and the cor anglais
  ত This instrument is named after its inventor, the German instrument-maker Wilhelm Heckel.

hederigerent
adjective
bearing or ornamented with ivy

helot
noun
a member of a class of serfs in ancient Sparta
  ত Helots were neither slaves nor freemen; they were bound to the land but owned by the state rather than an individual.

hemistich
noun
1 a half-line or section of a line of verse, especially where separated from the rest of the line by a caesura or similar device
2 an incomplete line of verse

hemitery
noun
a malformation or deformity, usually congenital

henotic
adjective
promoting harmony; unifying; irenic
ह्ल्ल The word is derived from Greek *heis* 'one'.

herdwick
noun
a tract of land used for pasturing sheep and in the charge of a herd, or shepherd, appointed by the landowner or lord of the manor
ह्ल्ल This word is better-known nowadays as the name of a breed of hardy Lakeland sheep.

herigaut
noun
an outer garment covering the upper body and resembling a cape with armholes and occasionally hanging sleeves which were decorative and not worn
ह्ल्ल The word was probably pronounced '*he*-ri-gowt', with the stress on the first syllable.

hermeneutics
noun
1 the interpretation and understanding of texts, especially of Scripture or literary texts
2 (in psychology) a method used to study human beings in society

hetaerism or hetairism
noun
1 concubinage
2 a social system in which a tribe practises communal marriage

heteric
adjective
(of word spellings) not phonetic

heteronym

noun

(in grammar) a word that has the same spelling as another word but a different pronunciation and meaning

> ꝰ The word is derived from Greek *heteros* 'other' and *onyma* 'name'. Examples of such words in English are 'bow', 'lead' and 'second'.

heuristic

noun

1 a technique that directs the attention in learning, discovery or problem-solving; in education, a teaching method that encourages or trains pupuls to work out solutions for themselves
2 (in computing) a method of solving a problem by using exploration and trial and error, rather than a fixed set of rules
adjective
relating to how something is discovered

heyduck or hayduck or haiduk

noun

1 a brigand
2 (in 16th- and 17th-century Hungary) an irregular or mercenary soldier who subsequently became a landowner and noble
3 (in 18th-century Poland) the liveried servant of a noble

hiaqua

noun

an ornament made from tooth-shells, or tooth-shells used as currency, by Native Indians on the north Pacific coast of North America

hierodule

noun

(in the ancient world) a slave living in a temple and dedicated to the service of a deity

hilo

noun
a thin vein of ore

hinny
noun
1 the offspring of a male horse and female donkey
2 (in Scotland and north-east England) darling, sweetheart

hippodame
noun
a horse-tamer

hodiernal
adjective
relating to the present day

homonomous
adjective
(in biology) denoting parts that are similar in structure or form and arranged in a series, eg fingers and toes

homunculus, homuncule or homuncle
noun
a diminutive man
> ৈ I particularly like the portly, musical sound of *homunculus*, and the definition of this word in *The Chambers Dictionary* is quite fascinating: 'a tiny man capable of being produced artificially according to Paracelsus, endowed with magical insight and power; a dwarf, manikin; a dwarf of normal proportions; a minute human form believed by the spermatist school of preformationists to be contained in the spermatozoon'.

horehound or hoarhound
noun
a herbaceous plant of the mint family
> ৈ The word is derived from Old English *hare* meaning 'hoary' and *hune* meaning 'plant'.

hornswoggle
verb
to cheat, deceive or hoax
> ৈ Originally North American slang, the origin of this word is unknown.

horst

noun

(in geology) a block of the Earth's crust that is higher than the surrounding land because faults on each side have forced the block upwards or caused the ground around it to subside

&ep; The word is German, meaning 'upheaval'.

housty

noun

a sore throat

hubris

noun

arrogance, over-confidence

&ep; In Greek tragedy, *hybris* was the excessive pride or defiance of the gods by a character which provoked retribution from the gods and led to his downfall.

huff-snuff

noun

a braggart; a conceited would-be swashbuckler

&ep; This very satisfying reduplicative word captures the very essence of a vain and boastful individual who is always quick to criticize. Being equally quick to take offence and harbour resentment, they shall therefore remain nameless.

hui or hoe or hoey or huey

noun

a Chinese secret society, especially one formed among Chinese migrants in another country

humicubation

noun

the act or habit of lying on the ground, eg in penitence, self-abasement

&ep; The word is derived from Latin *humus* 'soil' and *cubare* 'to lie down'.

hummum
noun
a place for sweating; a sweating bath such as a Turkish bath

hygeiolatry
noun
an obsession with health or hygiene

hygroma
noun
a swelling, such as a cyst or tumour, that contains a serous fluid but not pus

hypnagogic or hypnogogic
adjective
1 inducing sleep; soporific
2 relating to the state of drowsiness that precedes sleep
  ঽ The word is derived from Greek *hypnos* 'sleep' and *agogos* 'leading'.

hypostasize or hypostatize
verb
to represent as a real entity; to embody; to personify

hypothecation
noun
a generic term for the use of property to secure a loan without transferring possession of the property; a pledge; a mortgage

hysteresis
noun
(in physics) the delay between the cause of an effect and the manifestation of the effect; it applies especially in the case of magnetization

Ii

iatrogenic
adjective
(of a patient's disease or symptom) caused unintentionally by the medical treatment or the actions or comments of the physician
> ﹖ The word is derived from Greek *iatros* 'physician' and *genesis* 'production'.

iconoclastic
adjective
1 relating to opposition to or an attack on traditional or cherished beliefs
2 relating to opposition to the use of religious images in worship or the destruction of religious images
> ﹖ The word is derived via Latin from ecclesiastical Greek *eikon* 'image, likeness' and *klastes* 'breaker'.

idiocrasy
noun
a characteristic, mental or emotional outlook, or behaviour that is peculiar to a person; idiosyncrasy

ier-oe or heir-oye
noun
a great-grandchild
> ﹖ This is a Scots word, derived from Gaelic *iar* 'after' and *ogha* 'grandchild'.

imago
noun
1 (in zoology) the final, fully developed stage of an insect after all metamorphoses are completed
2 (in psychology) an often idealized mental picture of oneself or someone else, usually formed in childhood and persisting into adult life

ઠ෴ This word comes from Latin where it means 'likeness'. It is pronounced 'i-*may*-goh' or 'i-*mah*-goh', with the stress on the second syllable.

imbricate
verb
(in biology) to overlap or be overlapped like roof tiles, eg leaves, feathers, fish scales, tissue, teeth, etc
adjective
having leaves, scales, etc overlapped in this way

ઠ෴ This word is derived from Latin *imbricare* 'to cover with rain-tiles'.

immanent
adjective
1 existing or remaining within something; inherent
2 (of a supreme being or power) permanently present throughout the universe

immorigerous
adjective
rude, boorish; obstinate; disobedient

imprecation
noun
a spoken curse, or the act of uttering a curse

inamorata (*feminine*) or inamorato (*masculine*)
noun
a person who is loved; a lover

ઠ෴ This affectionate term is derived from Italian *innamorare* 'to cause to fall in love' from Latin *amor* 'love'.

inanition

noun

emptiness, especially physical exhaustion owing to lack of nourishment as a consequence of starvation or disease

incarnadine

adjective

1 flesh-coloured

2 crimson; blood-red

verb

to make flesh-coloured; to redden

> ❧ Perhaps the most familiar use of this verb comes from Act II of *Macbeth*, when, after murdering Duncan, a tortured Macbeth fears that he will never be cleansed of his victim's blood: 'Will all great Neptune's ocean wash this blood / Clean from my hand? No, this my hand will rather / The multitudinous seas incarnadine, / Making the green one red.'

incensory

noun

a vessel in which incense is burnt; a censer

inchoate

adjective

at the initial point or in an early stage of development; rudimentary, undeveloped, unformed, immature

verb

to begin, or cause to begin

> ❧ The word is usually pronounced 'in-*koh*-ayt', with the stress on the second syllable.

inchpin

noun

the sweetbread of a deer

incipit

noun

the beginning or first words or lines of a text in a manuscript or early printed book

• The word is derived from Latin *incipere* 'to begin'. The third person singular in the present tense, *incipit* 'here beginneth', was used by medieval scribes to indicate the start of a new division in a manuscript. It can be pronounced either 'in-*sip*-it' or 'in-*kip*-it', with the stress on the second syllable.

incrispated
adjective
stiffly curled; wrinkled

incunabulum
noun
1 an early printed book, especially one printed before 1501
2 (in plural) the early stages or first signs of development of something

• The origin of this word is both pleasing and fascinating. It derives from Latin *incunabula* meaning 'swaddling clothes', from *in*- 'in' and *cunae* 'cradle', and as such neatly refers to the infancy of printing. The first documented use of 'incunabulum' as a printing term occurs in the early 1600s but by the end of the century the term (and its plural form 'incunabula') was being used to describe early printed works themselves.

indefesse
adjective
unwearied, untiring

ineffable
adjective
1 indescribable; too great to be expressed in words
2 not meant or not allowed to be said, usually because the words are perceived to be too sacred

ineluctable
adjective
not able to be resisted, evaded or escaped from

infauna

noun
the aquatic animal life found in the sediments on an ocean floor, river bed, etc

infundibular

adjective
1 funnel-shaped
2 having a funnel
  ࣃ❧ The word is derived from Latin *infundere* 'to pour in'.

ingénue

noun
1 an unsophisticated young woman
2 (in the theatre) the part of an unsophisticated young woman in a play, or the actress who plays such a role

ingrate

noun
an ungrateful person
adjective
ungrateful

inkie-pinkie or (h)inky-pinky

noun
1 small beer, ie of a weak, poor or inferior quality
2 a stew made from cold roast beef and vegetables
3 nonsense words used in children's rhymes
  ࣃ❧ This is a Scots word of unknown origin.

innascible

adjective
without a beginning; not subject to the condition of birth
  ࣃ❧ In Christian theology this word is applied to God the Father.

inspissate

verb
to thicken; to condense

interbastation

noun
patchwork quilting

intercalate

verb
1 to insert a day or month into the calendar to harmonize it with the solar year
2 to insert or interpose anything out of the ordinary

intersilient

adjective
suddenly emerging in the midst of something

interstice

noun
a small or narrow space between things, especially parts of the body

inthronistic

adjective
relating to an ordination
noun
a gift made to a bishop for an ordination or installation, usually a sum of money intended to defray his expenses

involucrum

noun
an envelope or enveloping sheath

involument

noun
a covering; an envelope

invultuation or invultation

noun
the making of a likeness of a person, usually in wax, for the purposes of witchcraft, voodoo, etc

inwick

noun
(in the game of curling) a shot that strikes the inside of another stone and glances off it towards the tee

irade

noun
an edict, especially one issued by a sultan

irenic or irenical

adjective
tending or intended to create peace

irredentist

noun
a person who favours the recovery by his or her country of territory that used to belong to it

    The word is derived from the Italian phrase *Italia irredenta* 'unredeemed Italy', the philosophy and policies underlying the 19th-century drive to unify all Italian-speaking areas into one state.

ithyphallic

noun
1 a poetic metre used in hymns to Bacchus, or a poem composed in this metre
2 a poem of a licentious nature
adjective
1 (in the ancient world) relating to the phallus carried in procession at the festivals of Bacchus
2 indecent; obscene; salacious
3 (in painting or sculpture) having an erect penis

Jj

jackaroo or jackeroo
noun
a novice hand on an Australian sheep- or cattle-station
   🐍 The female equivalent of a 'jackaroo' is a 'jillaroo'.

jactation or jactitation
noun
1 (in civil law) the offence of falsely, maliciously and publicly claiming to be married to someone
2 (in medicine) the restless tossing and twitching of a seriously ill person
   🐍 The word is derived from Latin *jactitare* 'to throw out publicly'.

jaculiferous
adjective
having spiky, arrow-like prickles

jettage
noun
dues levied on vessels for the use of a jetty or pier in a port, especially at Hull

jhula or joolah
noun
1 (in Himalayan areas of northern India) a suspension bridge, originally made of rope and in modern times of wire cables or iron

2 a swing or swinging seat

ৡ✈ The word is derived from Hindi *jhula* 'swing, swing-rope'.

jim-jams

noun

1 a state of nervousness or febrile excitement

2 (slang) delirium tremens

3 (colloquial) pyjamas

jobation

noun

a scolding; a lengthy, tedious reproof

jorum

noun

a large drinking bowl

ৡ✈ The word is believed to be derived from the Old Testament character Joram, who brought vessels made of precious metals to King David (2 Samuel 8.10). 'Jorum' also came to be applied to the contents of the bowl.

jouk or juke

verb

(in football) a deceptive move by a player; a dodge; a feint

ৡ✈ The word is derived from Middle English *jowken* 'to bend in a supple way'.

jussel

noun

a dish made of various ingredients mixed into a broth; a hotch-potch

ৡ✈ The word is derived via Old French *jussel* 'juice, broth' from Latin *ius* 'broth, soup'.

kakistocracy

noun

a system of government in which the rulers are the least competent, least qualified or most unprincipled citizens

   ફ્◆ Although this method of selection of rulers and government is not known to have officially existed at any time in history, 'kakistocracy' is certainly a very expressive and useful word, easy as it is to apply to any number of governments through history and around the world.

kalgan

noun

a fur obtained from Kalgan lamb

   ફ્◆ The fur is named after the city of Kalgan (now Zhangjiakou) in north-eastern China.

kalopsia

noun

a condition in which things appear more beautiful than they really are

   ફ્◆ Derived from the Greek terms *kallos*, meaning 'beautiful', and *opsis*, meaning 'sight', this might be a suitable word to remember when we wonder at our friends' and relations' new partner, their irksome children or even their smelly and incontinent yet beloved old pet. Indeed, recent scientific research carried out by neuroscientists at University College London seems to bear out the old proverb 'love is blind' by demonstrating that both romantic and maternal love suppress brain activity associated with criticism and negative feelings. Potentially more dangerous is the kalopsia experienced in the form of 'beer goggles' after a few too many drinks.

kankie
noun
a West African bread made from maize-flour

kelpie
noun
1 (in Scottish folklore) a malignant water spirit, usually in the form of a horse, that tries to cause travellers to drown
2 a breed of Australian sheepdog
  ɞ The malicious, shape-shifting kelpies of Scottish folklore were believed to haunt fresh water rivers, fords and streams. Either in the guise of a handsome young man, or a beautiful horse offering a dry crossing, the kelpie would tempt weary travellers to their deaths in treacherous waters. The practical James Headrick, in his *General View of the Agriculture of the County of Angus* (1813), reports frankly, 'The water kelpie, a mischievous being who was supposed to frequent the rivers, and who first seduced the unwary into the stream, and then carried them off to sea, has fallen into oblivion since bridges were constructed in all convenient places.'

kenspeckle or kenspeck
noun
(in Scottish and northern English dialect) conspicuous; easily recognized

kiddlywink or kiddleywink
noun
a public house selling beer and cider, found especially in Cornwall
  ɞ The type of ale house known as a 'kiddlywink' or 'kiddleywink' was established around 1830, although the etymology of the term is unknown. Described by commentators of the time as 'low' with infamously rough wares on sale, the sweet-sounding name belied a disorderly reality, one which was certainly not a place for 'kiddywinks'.

kinker
noun
(in the USA) a circus performer
  ʒ Originally the word denoted an acrobat.

kip
noun
a move or manoeuvre in gymnastics in which the hip joint is
extended quickly to give the body momentum

kissel or keessel
noun
a Russian dessert made with fruit juice, sugar and water, thickened
with cornflour or another form of starch

kramat
noun
a Muslim shrine or place of pilgrimage, usually the tomb of a man of
notable piety
adjective
holy, sacred

Kufic or Cufic
adjective
relating to Kufa, an ancient city near Babylon (both in modern Iraq)
and a seat of Islamic learning
  ʒ The word is applied especially to an angular form of Arabic script
believed to originate with scholars in the city.

kwedini
noun
a South African boy or young man, especially one that has not yet
undergone the ritual circumcision that is the rite of passage to
manhood

Ll

labarum
noun
1 a symbolic banner, especially one carried in ecclesiastical processions
2 the imperial standard adopted by the Roman emperor Constantine the Great after his conversion, on which Christian symbols were added to Roman military symbols

labey
noun
1 (in Scots dialect) a flap or skirt of a garment
2 a loose garment or wrap
> This word is believed to be derived from Gaelic *leàbag* 'flap'.

lachrymose
adjective
1 (of a person) given to frequent bouts of crying; having a tendency to cry with little provocation
2 (of a book, film, play, etc) sad; likely to induce tears

laevorotatory or levorotatory
adjective
rotating to the left or anticlockwise

lagan
noun
(in law) goods left in the sea on a wreck, or thrown overboard attached to a float or buoy before the vessel sinks so that they can be recovered later

lapactic
adjective
purgative; laxative

lapidate
verb
to put to death by stoning
→ The word is derived from Latin *lapis* 'stone'.

lapidose
adjective
having an abundance of stones; stony

lastage
noun
1 a duty exacted from traders attending a market or fair for rights of carriage; also, a tax on the goods sold there
2 the lading of a ship; ballast

latifundium
noun
a great landed estate, usually specializing in large-scale agriculture for export
→ The word is derived from Latin *latus* 'broad, spacious' and *fundus* 'farm, estate'. Originally applied to such estates in the Roman Empire, the term is also used of large estates in modern Spain and Latin America. The word 'latifundian' means 'possessing a large estate'.

lation
noun
motion from one place to another; transportation; conveyance

latrability

noun
the ability to bark

leam

noun
a ray, flash or gleam of light
verb
to shine; to gleam

ledgit

noun
1 (in Scots dialect) a small shelf
2 a label projecting from the page of a book

legerdemain

noun
1 sleight of hand; conjuring tricks or juggling
2 trickery; sophistry
> The word is derived from French *léger de main* 'light of hand,
  dexterous'. In English, the word is pronounced 'lej-uh-duh-*mayn*', with
  the stress on the fourth syllable, although the French pronunciation
  'lezh-air-duh-manh' is also heard.

leman

noun
a sweetheart or lover
> The word is derived from Middle English *leofman*, from *leof* 'dear' and
  man 'man'. It was occasionally applied to a husband or wife, but usually
  the relationship referred to was outside marriage.

lenic

adjective
pertaining to a metal instrument used for pressing and moulding coal

lenity

noun
mercifulness, mildness

lestercock

noun

a dummy sailing boat carried out to sea by the wind with a long fishing line of baited hooks attached, and drawn back in by a cord tied or anchored on land

> ৯ The word is derived from Old Cornish *lester* 'a ship' and *coc* 'a (small ship's) boat'. This method of fishing was used when the weather was too rough for fishing boats to put to sea.

lestrigon

noun

a cannibal

> ৯ The word is derived via Latin from Greek *Laestrygones* 'skin-reapers, raw-hide gatherers'. It is an Anglicization of Laestrygonians, a tribe of cannabalistic giants encountered by Odysseus on his way home from Troy, according to Homer's *Odyssey*.

lethologica

noun

the inability to remember a word or call to mind the right word

> ৯ This unfairly complicated word, which seems to beg for a simpler, everyday alternative, is the correct term to describe an extremely common condition. It derives from Greek *lethe* 'forgetfulness' and *logos* 'word'.

librate

verb

1 to vibrate before coming to a total rest; to oscillate; hence, to poise, or balance

2 to determine the weight of; to put in the balance

> ৯ The word is derived from Latin *librare* 'to balance, make even'.

limaceous

adjective

relating to the genus *Limax*, or the slugs; slug-like

limicolous
adjective
living in mud

litham
noun
a veil covering the lower part of the face, worn by some Muslim women and by the men of some Saharan nomadic tribes, such as the Tuareg

litten
noun
a churchyard
> ॐ The word is derived from Old English *líc* 'corpse' and *tún* 'enclosure'.

Loiner
noun
an inhabitant of Leeds, West Yorkshire

lollop
verb
to move in an energetic but ungainly way

loogan
noun
(US slang) a foolish or unsophisticated fellow

lubricious
adjective
1 lewd, prurient
2 slippery, smooth, oily

lucripetous
adjective
eager for gain; avaricious; grasping
> ॐ The word is pronounced 'loo-*krip*-it-us', with the stress on the second syllable.

lucubrate
verb
1 to write or study, especially at night
2 to produce scholarly or literary writings; to clarify or expand on a discourse in a learned way

&❧ This archaic word is derived from Latin *lucubrare* meaning 'to work by lamplight' and describes a concept with which I became very familiar during my time at school. I was obliged to spend many hours lucubrating in order to produce my scholarly writings, all of which were scrupulously left until the last minute.

lunker
noun
an animal, especially a fish, that is a large example of its species; a 'whopper'

lupanarian
adjective
pertaining to a brothel

lusher
noun
someone who indulges themselves to excess, especially in drink

lycanthropy
noun
1 the supposed magical transformation of a human into a wolf
2 (in psychiatry) a delusion of being a wolf

&❧ The word is derived from Greek *lykos* 'wolf' and *anthropos* 'man', which also provide the term 'lycanthrope' meaning either 'a werewolf' or 'a sufferer of lycanthropy'.

lyfkie
noun
a bodice

&❧ The word was probably pronounced '*leef*-kee', with the stress on the first syllable.

Mm

Macassar

adjective

relating to the port of Macassar (now Makassar) in Indonesia

 ❧ The port gave its name to the wood of the ebony tree found in the region (and also in India and Sri Lanka). The popular 19th-century hair oil which also takes its name from the port was originally composed of the oil of the Ceylon oak and perfumed with ylang-ylang flowers. The widespread use of this intensely pungent oil demanded the invention of the 'antimacassar' – a fabric covering used to protect the backs of chairs and sofas from greasy stains.

macédoine

noun

1 a mixture of fruit or vegetables, usually diced and sometimes jellied
2 a mixture

 ❧ The word is French, meaning 'Macedonia'. It was probably coined because of the mixture of ethnic groups in that region.

maceration

noun

1 the process of softening or breaking up something by soaking it in water
2 the process of becoming emaciated through fasting

machicolation
noun
a space between the corbels supporting a parapet, or an opening in the floor of a projecting gallery, which extended beyond curtain walls of castles and city walls and through which missiles, stones, boiling oil, etc could be dropped onto an attacking enemy

> ❧ The word, pronounced 'muh-chik-uh-*lay*-shun', with the stress on the fourth syllable, is derived from Latin, via Provençal *macar*, meaning 'crush', and *col*, meaning 'neck'. Another type of machicolation, found in internal gallery and gateway ceilings, was known less ceremoniously as a 'murder hole'.

macrology
noun
1 lengthy and tedious talk expressing little of substance; a superfluity of words
2 (in computer hacking slang) a set of complex, or poorly built and over-complex, macros

> ❧ A word which I find useful to remember in a world populated by politicians and public figures who talk freely while saying little or nothing. An anonymous definition for 'committee' springs to mind: 'a group of people who take minutes and waste hours'.

majuscule
noun
1 a large letter used as the first letter of the word in writing or printing proper names; a capital letter; an upper-case letter
2 large lettering
adjective
of or written in large lettering

makutu
noun
(in New Zealand and Polynesia) witchcraft, a magic spell

malabathrum or malobathrum
noun
1 the leaf of an oriental plant of the genus *Cinnamomum*, or the

fragrant oil prepared from these leaves

2 the dried leaves of this or related plants

> ৡৠ The oil was much prized by the ancient Greeks and Romans, while the dried leaves were used in medicines in medieval Europe. The word is pronounced 'mal-uh-*bath*-rum', with the stress on the third syllable.

malversation

noun

1 corrupt behaviour in a position of trust

2 corrupt administration, especially of public funds

> ৡৠ The word is derived from Latin *male* 'badly' and *versari* 'to behave oneself'.

mandative

adjective

(in grammar) conveying a command or calling for a particular action

manducate

verb

to chew, masticate; to eat

mantelet or mantlet

noun

1 a woman's short, sleeveless cape or short, fitted coat, popular in the 19th century

2 (in warfare) a large mobile shield or screen providing protection against missiles in medieval times; in tanks etc, the armour plate shielding the opening through which the gun barrel projects from the hull armour

manumit

verb

to release someone from slavery; to set someone free

> ৡৠ The word is derived from Latin *manumittere* 'to send from one's hand or control'.

marc

noun

1 the residue of skins, stems, etc left over after grapes have been pressed

2 a brandy made from this residue

mardy

adjective

sulky; whining (usually of a child)

> ಶ A word which is described as northern English dialect in most dictionaries but with which many people will be familiar from their childhood. Presumably the meaning was unknown to the parents of the American tennis player Mardy Fish when they christened their child. In the United Kingdom, there are two small towns which glory in the name of Mardy, one in Monmouthshire and the other in Shropshire.

maritodespotism

noun

the domination of a wife by her husband through the use of fear or force

marmoreal

adjective

resembling marble, or made of marble

masdeu

noun

a fortified red wine made in southern France

> ಶ This wine enjoyed a brief but intense popularity in Britain in Victorian times.

materteral

adjective

like or of an aunt

> ಶ The word is pronounced 'muh-*tur*-tuh-rul', with the stress on the second syllable.

mathesis
noun
1 learning or science, especially mathematics
2 the action of learning; mental application, discipline
 {:> The word is Greek, meaning 'science'.

matross
noun
(in the British army) a soldier who helped artillery gunners in loading, firing, sponging and moving cannon and other guns
 {:> The word is derived from German *Matrosen* 'seamen', because a matross's duties were considered sailors' work. The rank in the British army was abolished in the late 18th century.

matutinal
adjective
1 relating to or occurring in the morning
2 early
 {:> The word is derived from Latin *matutinus* 'of the morning', from Matuta, a Roman goddess of the dawn.

melisma
noun
(in music) a passage in which several notes are sung to one syllable of the text

mell
noun
1 (Scots, English and Irish dialect) any type of heavy hammer or mallet, including those used for laundry and athletic contests
2 (Scots dialect) a heavy blow, such as that given by a large hammer
3 honey

mellisonant
adjective
sweet-sounding; pleasing to the ear; dulcet
 {:> This beautiful-sounding word (with an equally appealing definition) is aptly derived from the Latin *mel* 'honey' and *sonare* 'to sound'.

membranaceous
adjective
1 relating to, resembling or made of a membrane
2 thin and pliable, like the leaf of certain trees and shrubs

mendaciloquent
adjective
telling lies; speaking falsehoods
⁂ The word is pronounced 'men-duh-*sil*-uh-kwent', with the stress on the third syllable.

menseful
adjective
1 (of people) well-behaved, polite, sensible, discreet, intelligent; good-mannered, hospitable
2 (of things) proper, seemly, decorous, respectable-looking
⁂ This is a northern English, Scots and Ulster dialect word, derived ultimately from the Old Norse *mennska* 'humanity, kindness'.

mentagra
noun
an inflammation of the hair follicles of the bearded part of men's faces, causing rashes of pimples

mentalese
noun
a hypothetical 'language' in which thoughts are represented in the mind without expression in words

mephitis
noun
1 a foul smell; a stench
2 a noxious, foul-smelling gas, especially one emanating from the earth

meracious
adjective
undiluted; unadulterated; full-strength; pungent

meson
noun
1 (in Mexico and southern USA) an inn, tavern or restaurant
2 (in particle physics) one of a group of unstable, strongly interacting subatomic particles
3 (in entomology) the mid-line of the body

mesonoxian
adjective
pertaining to midnight

metanoia
noun
the process of changing one's mind or opinion, especially where this is accompanied by a change of conduct, eg repentence and conversion

mew
noun
1 a cage or other quarters for hawks, especially when they are moulting
2 a secret place; a place of concealment, retirement or confinement
verb
1 to confine, coop up, conceal
2 (of a hawk) to moult
   The word 'mews' came to be used of stabling for horses because royal stables were built on the site of hawks' mews at Charing Cross in London.

miasma
noun
1 a thick vapour, especially one given off by a swamp, marsh, etc, and believed to be poisonous or infectious
2 an unpleasant or evil influence or atmosphere
   The word is derived from Greek, meaning 'pollution'.

micturition
noun
(in medicine) urination

mill-scale
noun
a thick coating of iron oxide formed on iron or steel during the hot rolling process

mimetic
adjective
1 relating to or practising imitation or mimicry
2 (in biology) showing a close resemblance to another animal, plant or inanimate object

minatory
adjective
threatening

minutious
adjective
concerned with and attentive to minutiae

mithridatize
verb
to develop a tolerance of or immunity to a poison by taking gradually larger doses of it

ᐓ The word is derived from the ancient king Mithridates IV of Pontus, who is supposed to have followed this practice.

mittle
verb
(in Scots dialect) to hurt, injure, maul or mutilate
noun
a hurt, injury, scar or weal

mna or mina
noun
a unit of weight and currency used in Greece and the Middle East in ancient times

mneme

noun

the ability of an organism or substance to retain a memory of the past experiences, patterns of behaviour or cultural practices or ideas of its own and past generations and to transmit these to future generations

 ↝ In early Greek mythology, Mneme was the Muse of memory. The 'm' is silent, and the word is pronounced '*nee*-mee', rhyming with 'creamy'.

moff

noun

a silk fabric from the Caucasus

mofussil

noun

(in India) those parts of the country outside the cities, or the rural areas of a district outside its main town

adjective

relating to the mofussil; rural, provincial

 ↝ The term originally applied to any area outside the three capitals – Mumbai (Bombay), Kolkata (Calcutta) and Chennai (Madras) – of the three Presidencies of the East India Company.

moiety

noun

a half; one of two parts or divisions

molendinaceous

adjective

(in botany) resembling the sails of a windmill

 ↝ The word is derived from Latin *molendinum* 'a mill', from *molere* 'to grind'.

mollag

noun

an inflated dog's skin used as a buoy or to float fishing nets

 ↝ The word is Manx, meaning 'buoy' or 'float', and it also occurs in various forms in regions of Britain where fishing was a major industry and there were Celtic influences on the dialect.

momism
noun
1 excessive devotion to one's mother
2 excessive mothering; over-protectiveness
   > The word was coined by an American writer and is derived from 'mom', the North American colloquialism for 'mother'.

monism
noun
1 (in philosopy) a theory that reality exists in only one form, with no duality between the physical and the spiritual
2 (in philosophy and theology) a belief in the existence of only one supreme being
   > The word is derived from Greek *monos* 'single'.

monstrance
noun
(in the Roman Catholic Church) a large open or transparent cup in which the consecrated host (eucharistic bread) is shown to the congregation during Mass
   > The word is derived from Latin *monstrare* 'to show'.

moodle
verb
to mooch; to meander aimlessly; to pass time in doing nothing

mowburn
verb
to heat up or ferment in the mow, eg hay or corn when stacked while too green

mucilage
noun
1 a sticky substance secreted by some plants and used as a type of adhesive
2 a sticky substance prepared from the roots, seeds, etc of certain plants for use as a tisane, poultice or adhesive
3 a gelatinous, semi-fluid mass; a pulp

Muggletonian

noun

a member of a religious sect (now defunct) that flourished in the 17th and 18th centuries

> ࣰ The sect was named after Ludovic Muggleton, a tailor whom his followers considered to be prophetic.

mum-chance

adjective

silent, unspeaking

> ࣰ The word is derived from the dice game of mumchance, which was played in silence.

mundungus

noun

a foul-smelling type of tobacco

> ࣰ The word is derived from Spanish *mondongo* 'tripe'.

mung

verb

1 (in Scots and English dialect) to mix; to muddle; to confuse
2 (in computing) to destroy a file etc by making extensive and eventually irreversible changes

murcid

adjective

1 lazy
2 shirking
3 cowardly

murcous

adjective

lacking a thumb

> ࣰ The word is derived from Latin *murcus* 'mutilated, truncated'. It came to be applied to those who avoided military service by cutting off one of their thumbs.

murken
verb
1 to darken, to grow dark; to become overcast
2 to make dark; to obscure

murmuration
noun
1 a low, continuous, indistinct sound; the act of murmuring
2 a flock of starlings
> ૐ Collective nouns denoting groups of people and animals have for many years been a popular area of study and debate; the coining of potential new words is an amusing offshoot of this. Accordingly, some of the newer terms, like 'a murmuration of starlings', are widely regarded as dubious. These include 'an abomination of monks', 'a pandemonium of parrots' and 'a turmoil of porpoises'. Terms which are officially recognized include 'a cete of badgers', 'an exaltation of larks' and 'a gam of whales'.

muscid
noun
a fly of the family Muscidae
adjective
relating to the Muscidae family

myrmidon
noun
1 a hired thug
2 a faithful servant who is prepared to be unscrupulous
3 a follower
> ૐ The word is derived from the Myrmidons, Thessalian warriors who went to the Trojan War with Achilles, according to Homer's *Iliad*.

Nn

nacreous
adjective
1 of or relating to mother-of-pearl
2 iridescent

nagsman
noun
a man or woman particularly skilled in handling and training horses, especially one employed to train and show them

naphthalic
adjective
relating to or derived from naphthalene, a white crystalline substance distilled from coal tar and used in mothballs and dye-making

narcosis
noun
1 the effects of soporific drugs, often including drowsiness or unconsciousness
2 a state of insensibility

nasel or nasal
noun
the part of a helmet which extended over the nose to protect it from injury

Nastalik or Nasta'liq

noun

a type of script in which Arabic may be written

    ह This script was developed in Persia by mixing the Nashki and Taliq
       scripts.

nasute

adjective

1 having a keen or discerning sense of smell

2 captious; cavilling

3 nose-like; having a large nose

    ह The word is usually pronounced '*nay*-zyoot', with the stress on the first
       syllable. It is derived from Latin *nasus* 'nose'.

nauscopy

noun

the ability to discern the approach of ships or land from a
considerable distance

nebshaft

noun

1 countenance; face

2 likeness; image

nekton

noun

marine and freshwater animals able to swim and move independently
of currents

    ह The word is derived via German from Greek *nechein* 'to swim'.

nemertean or nemertine

noun

any member of the phylum Nemertea, worms with long, flat,
unsegmented bodies that live in the sea or in tidal mud flats

adjective

relating to this phylum of worms

neologism

noun

1 a new word or expression
2 a new meaning acquired by an existing word or expression
3 the practice of coining or introducing neologisms

neomenia

noun

the time of the new moon; the beginning of a month in a lunar calendar

nerf

verb

1 to bump or push another car, especially in drag-racing
2 to participate in war-game activities using mock weapons that fire foam ammunition
3 (in multi-player online games) to reduce the power of a weapon or skill

Nesselrode

noun

a rich pudding made from chestnut puree, candied and dried fruits, and maraschino liqueur or rum, mixed with custard and made into ice cream

    꿍 This elaborate dessert is said to have been devised in 1814 in honour of Russian diplomat Count Karl Nesselrode. The chef responsible for the recipe is not known for sure, but is believed by some to have been the architect of haute cuisine, Antoine Carême. Ice puddings at this time were technically very difficult to prepare and were therefore particularly favoured amongst the upper classes of Victorian society; the rich, extravagant Nesselrode pudding was considered the highest achievement of the genre.

neurasthenia

noun

a condition characterized by fatigue, anxiety, listlessness and non-specific physical symptoms

    꿍 This obsolete medical term was derived from Greek *neuron* 'nerve' and *asthenes* 'weak'.

neve
noun
a mark on the skin

newel
noun
1 the central post of a flight of stairs that supports winding stairs
2 the top or bottom post supporting a stair-rail
> ?➤ The word is derived via Old French *nouel* 'knob' from Latin *nodellus*, a diminutive of *nodus* 'knot'.

nexal
adjective
1 relating to or typical of a nexus, especially in grammar
2 (in Roman law) relating to or typical of a nexum, a binding arrangement by which a creditor could recover a debt by selling the defaulting debtor as a slave

nidge
verb
(in building) to dress a stone roughly with a sharp-pointed hammer

nidulation
noun
the period of remaining in the nest

nifle
noun
a trifle

nigget or nidget
noun
a small insect, especially one that is the familiar of a witch
> ?➤ *The Chambers Dictionary* defines a familiar as 'a spirit or demon supposed to come to a person, especially a witch, at his or her call'. While I was aware of the more 'familiar' familiars, those taking the form of black cats, bats, owls and so on, I was surprised to discover

the strangely-named nigget, who somehow seems altogether more sinister and menacing than his larger colleagues.

nigon

noun
a stingy, miserly person; a niggard

nim

verb
1 to take
2 to steal, pilfer
→ The first sense of the verb, now archaic, may have given its name to the game of nim, in which two players take it in turns to remove an item from heaps or rows of small objects, each trying to take, or not take, the last item.

nimmer

noun
a petty thief

nipperkin

noun
1 a small drinking cup with a capacity believed to be about one eighth of a pint (*c.*70 ml)
2 a measure of wine or beer, believed to have been about one eighth of a pint
3 any small quantity
→ The word is probably derived from German or Dutch *nippen* 'to sip'.

nipshot

adverb
(in shooting) amiss in some way
→ The word occurs in the Scottish expression 'to play nipshot', said of an archer, cannon, etc.

nither

verb
1 to chill; to pinch, stunt or shrivel with cold or hunger; to straiten
2 to be shivery; to tremble with cold

၆► These meanings are the only ones to survive in modern Scots and English dialects from the original Old English, meaning 'to oppress, suppress, constrain', from Old Norse *niðra* 'to bring low, humiliate'.

nivation
noun
the processes whereby the ground beneath and next to banks of snow is eroded, forming a depression in the ground in which snow collects

noctivagous
adjective
wandering in the night

၆► This word, which derives from the Latin *nox* 'night', and *vagari* 'to wander', is pronounced 'nok-*tiv*-uh-gus', with the stress on the second syllable. Although I do not suffer from this affliction, I have fond memories of the Danish girlfriend of a close friend who was often to be found wandering naked into the rooms of others late at night, completely oblivious to her whereabouts, and who was charmingly unaware of her noctivagous adventures the next day.

nodose
adjective
knotty, knotted; having nodes or swellings

nome
noun
1 (in ancient Greece) a song or hymn to honour the gods
2 the musical and literary genre to which such songs belonged

no-nation
adjective
rough; uncouth; uncivilized; wild; lawless

nosean
noun
a mineral of the sodalite group found in igneous rock

၆► The word is pronounced '*noh*-zi-un', with the stress on the first syllable.

nosocomial

adjective
relating or belonging to a hospital
  ह The word is derived from Greek *nosos* 'disease' and *komeion* 'to tend'.

nosopoetic

adjective
producing or causing disease

nostrificate

verb
1 to recognize a degree or similar qualification awarded by a foreign university as equal to a native one
2 to have one's degree recognized in a foreign country

noumenon

noun
(in the philosophy of Immanuel Kant) the unknowable and indescribable reality of a thing in itself, which cannot be known through perception
  ह The word is derived via German from Greek *noein* 'to perceive by thought', from *nous* 'mind'.

novenary

adjective
of or relating to the number nine
  ह The word is derived from Latin *novem* 'nine'.

novercal

adjective
relating to or characteristic of a stepmother
  ह The word is pronounced 'noh-*vur*-kul', with the stress on the second syllable.

nowch

noun
1 a clasp or brooch
2 a setting for precious stones

3 a jewel or jewelled ornament worn on the person

    ع This is a variant spelling of 'nouch', which is an alteration of 'ouch', from a Germanic source meaning 'brooch'.

noxal

adjective

(in law) relating to wrongful injury or damage done by a person, animal or object belonging to another person

noyade

noun

the drowning of many persons at once, especially as a form of mass execution

nubecula

noun

1 (in astronomy) a nebula

2 (in medicine) a clouded spot on the cornea; a floater

3 a cloudy appearance in urine

    ع The word is derived from the Latin diminutive for *nubes* 'cloud'.

nuciferous

adjective

(in botany) bearing or producing nuts

nucivorous

adjective

(in zoology) nut-eating

    ع I love the sound and the idea of this word, which reminds me very much of Christmas-time.

nudnik or nudnick

noun

a boring or pestering person

    ع Derived from Yiddish *nudyen* meaning 'boring' and *-nik* 'a person associated with a particular quality', this word provides a most satisfying insult.

nugatory
adjective
1 of little or no importance or value; trifling
2 ineffective; futile; invalid
    ❧ The word is derived from Latin *nugae* 'jests', via *nugari* 'to trifle'.

nuggar or nugger
noun
a type of boat used on the River Nile, usually for carrying cargo

nullibiety
noun
the state or condition of being nowhere; absence
    ❧ The word is derived from Latin *nullibi* 'nowhere'.

nullipore
noun
any of various marine algae that secrete carbonate of lime on their surface

numinous
adjective
1 awe-inspiring; evoking a spiritual response
2 inducing a sense of a deity's presence
    ❧ The word is derived from Latin *numen* 'a presiding deity or spirit'.

nyctophonia
noun
a form of elective mutism in which someone or something is able or willing to speak only at night
    ❧ 'Nyctophoniac' creatures include owls and amorous cats.

Oo

obacerate
verb
to stop one's mouth, or that of someone else

obambulate
verb
to wander aimlessly

   ঌ Many Londoners will sympathize with the particular feelings of frustration one often encounters in those parts of the city which are popular with tourists. The prerequisite breakneck speed at which stressed-out Londoners must walk seems to be roughly twice that employed by our relaxed, holidaying visitors. 'Obambulation' is a wonderfully onomatopoeic word which so accurately describes the unhurried, random movements of the mass of bodies found, for example, on Portobello Road on Saturday mornings.

oblongitude
noun
oblong shape or form

obloquy
noun
1 being generally spoken of in an abusive or derogatory manner; calumny; vilification
2 a state of notoriety, disgrace or ill-repute resulting from abuse or detraction

obtemper

verb

to obey, submit to or comply with, especially a judgment, decree or order of a court of law

> ཨ Once in general use in Scotland, this word is now largely confined to its use in Scots law.

ochlophobia

noun

an abnormal fear of crowds

> ཨ The word is derived from Greek *ochlos* 'crowd' and *phobia* 'fear'.

oculogyric

adjective

1 relating to the turning of the eyes in the eye-socket
2 eye-rolling

> ཨ In medicine, an oculogyric crisis is a condition in which the eyeballs are fixed in an extreme position for a prolonged period of time.

oenomel

noun

(in ancient Greece) a drink made with unfermented grape juice and honey

> ཨ The word is pronounced '*een*-uh-mel', with the stress on the first syllable.

oenophilist

noun

a wine lover; a connoisseur of wine

og

noun

(Australian and New Zealand slang) a shilling

oleaginous

adjective

1 containing or producing oil; oil-like; oily, greasy
2 ingratiating, sycophantic, fawning

olecranon
noun
(in anatomy) the part of the upper end of the ulna that projects beyond the elbow joint and forms the outer part of the elbow
> ও The word is derived from Greek *olene* 'elbow' and *kranion* 'head'.

oligochaetology
noun
the study of annelid worms of the class Oligochaeta

onerable
adjective
burdensome; onerous

oniomania
noun
a compulsion to make purchases
> ও More commonly known as 'shopaholism', this is a term with which I have become familiar through the compulsion of various members of my female-dominated family to 'shop until they drop'. Thankfully their 'hobby' is yet to develop into the expensive and dangerous addiction a love of spending can become – an addiction often treated with specialized drugs and via dedicated groups such as 'shopaholics anonymous'.

ontology
noun
(in philosopy) the branch of metaphysics that deals with the nature and essence of existence
> ও The word is derived from Greek *onta* 'real things' and *logos* 'study'.

onychophagy or onychophagia
noun
the habit of biting one's fingernails
> ও The word is pronounced 'on-i-*kof*-uh-ji', with the stress on the third syllable.

ophelimity
noun
(in economics) the capacity to provide satisfaction

ophiolatry
noun
the worship of snakes
 ʇ The word is derived from Greek *ophis* 'snake' and *latreia* 'worship'.

opisthenar
noun
the back of the hand

oppilative
adjective
obstructive; tending to obstruct or stop up

opsony
noun
any food eaten along with bread

orihon
noun
a Japanese folding book, formed by folding the individual sheets of paper concertina-style

orming
adjective
ungainly; awkward; clumsy

orthogonal
adjective
right-angled; at right angles
 ʇ The word is derived from Greek *orthos* 'straight' and *gonia* 'angle'.

oscitancy
noun
the act of yawning, especially as a manifestation of drowsiness,
dullness or inattention

 ỡ The word is derived from Latin *oscitare* 'to yawn, gape', from *os* 'mouth'
 and *citare* 'to move'.

osotogari
noun
a type of leg throw in judo

ostreal
adjective
relating to oysters

otiose
adjective
1 futile
2 serving no purpose; functionless; superfluous
3 lazy; indolent

 ỡ The word is derived from Latin *otium* 'leisure'.

oubliette
noun
a secret dungeon with only one access point, usually hidden, through
a trapdoor at the top

 ỡ Derived from French *oublier* 'to forget', this misleadingly pretty
 and inoffensive-sounding word reveals a very unpleasant concept,
 and the startling ideology behind its use. During the recent major
 refurbishment of Foyles bookshop in Charing Cross Road, one of
 the biggest bookshops in the country, which has occupied the same
 building for nearly one hundred years, we explored passages and rooms
 in the labyrinthine interior which had lain unexplored for decades.
 Although we did not find any 'oubliettes' containing the forgotten
 remains of bygone book thieves, we did find a lift whose existence
 was a complete revelation to every member of staff.

Pp

pabulum
noun
1 a substance that can provide nourishment; food
2 bland or trivial intellectual activity or entertainment

pachisi
noun
a board game for four players which is similar to backgammon but uses six cowrie shells instead of dice
> ঌ The word is pronounced 'pah-*chee*-zi', rhyming with 'easy'. Variant spellings include 'parchesi' and 'parcheesi'. It is derived from Hindi *pachisi* 'twenty-five', the highest score that can be thrown in the game, which is thought to have originated in India and is common throughout south Asia.

pachydermatous
adjective
1 relating to or characteristic of a pachyderm, eg an elephant, rhinoceros
2 thick-skinned; insensitive; callous

padkos
noun
(in South Africa) food to eat on a journey

paizogony
noun
love play; petting

palimbacchius
noun
(in poetry) a metrical foot of two long and one short syllable

palimpsest
noun
1 an ancient writing material or manuscript that has been written upon more than once, the original writing having been erased
2 a monumental brass that has been turned over and inscribed on the reverse side

> The word is derived from Greek *palin* 'again' and *psestos* 'rubbed smooth'.

palindrome
noun
a word or phrase that reads the same backwards and forwards

> Like the acrostics and pangrams mentioned elsewhere in this collection, palindromes have amused writers and wordsmiths for centuries. The earliest known example was found as a graffito at Herculaneum, one of the towns destroyed in the aftermath of the eruption of Mount Vesuvius in AD 79. Perhaps the most famous palindromic phrase is 'A man, a plan, a canal – Panama!' devised by Leigh Mercer in the 1940s. With the help of computer programmes modern palindromists are able to take their craft to new heights – a version of the same palindrome devised in the 1980s with the help of a computer reached 544 words!

palinoia
noun
the compulsive repetition of an act until performed perfectly

> This neologism became widely known after it was used as part of a credit for an episode of the 1990s US animated television comedy *Pinky and the Brain*. My most memorable experience of the concept came during the filming of the TV series *Foyle's War*, in one episode of

which I had a speaking walk-on part as a bookseller. It is a testament to the patience and professionalism of actors, and the perseverance and perfectionism of directors, to observe how many times each scene was rehearsed and filmed before it was deemed perfect in every detail.

palpate
verb
to examine part of the body by touching or pressing it, usually to arrive at a medical diagnosis

panegyric
noun
a public speech or piece of writing in praise of someone or something or an achievement; a eulogy

    ɞ˩ The word is derived from Greek *panegyrikos* 'fit for a national festival', from *pan-* 'all' and *agyris* 'assembly'.

pangram
noun
a sentence that contains all the letters of the alphabet, ideally in the minimum number of words

    ɞ˩ Pangrams are not only a useful tool for typesetters and graphic designers, employed to display the properties of various fonts on the page, but also an ancient and diverting wordgame, known throughout the world in any number of languages. Perhaps the best-known pangram in English is, 'the quick brown fox jumped over the lazy dog', although, at 36 letters, it is by no means the shortest. 'Perfect pangrams', those which contain each letter of the alphabet only once, are extremely difficult to devise, and generally meaningless. Many contain nonsense words, initial letters and proper nouns, thoroughly undesirable amongst purists.

pantopod
noun
a marine arthropod of the class Pantopoda or Pycnogonida, such as sea spiders

paracme
noun
the stage following the highest point; hence, the period of life when one is past one's prime, or the point in a fever when the crisis is past

paradiastole
noun
1 (in rhetoric) a figure of speech which makes a negative quality appear positive
2 (in the Bible) a figure of speech which repeats disjunctions at the beginning of successive sentences or phrases

paralipomena or paraleipomena
noun
things omitted from a work and added as a supplement
   ঽ The word is derived via ecclesiastical Latin from Greek *paraleipein* 'to omit'. It is applied in particular to the books of Chronicles in the Old Testament, which cover similar events but contain details not found in the books of Samuel and Kings.

paralogism
noun
1 a fallacy
2 unintentionally illogical reasoning

parasang
noun
a unit of distance used in ancient Persia
   ঽ Originally a parasang was the distance that could be travelled in one hour and it is usually reckoned now to have been approximately three and a half miles.

paraselene
noun
a bright spot on the halo around the Moon, caused by light refracted from ice crystals; also called the 'mock moon'

pardine
adjective
relating to or resembling a pard, ie a leopard or other large cat; spotted

parergon
noun
1 work that is subordinate or subsidiary to a person's main employment
2 an accessory

parietal
adjective
1 (in anatomy) relating to or forming the wall of a body part, organ or cavity
2 (in botany) relating to or forming the wall of a hollow structure; borne on the inside of the ovary wall
3 (in USA) relating to residence within or having authority within a college

parisology
noun
the use, especially deliberately, of ambiguous words

paronomasia
noun
a play on words; a pun

> The word is derived from Greek *paronomazein* which means 'to call by a different name'. Perhaps the reason behind the relative obscurity of the term 'paronomasia', despite its everyday meaning, is the fact that 'pun' is so much punchier, so much easier to pronounce and quite easy to remember.

parorexia
noun
an appetite that is abnormal or craves items that are inappropriate as food

parp
noun
a honking sound, especially that of a car horn or of breaking wind
> ঌ I have a great fondness for imitative words, particularly the more down-to-earth examples such as 'plap', 'plop', 'parp', 'burp', 'squelch' and 'honk', which always seem to bring a smile to the face.

parse
verb
1 (in grammar) to analyse a sentence and describe its component parts
2 (in computational linguistics) to analyse a sentence or text and test its conformability with a given grammar
3 (in computing) to analyse a string of characters in terms of the computer language being used

pary
verb
1 to bet; to stake
2 to tally

pavis
noun
an oblong convex shield large enough to protect the whole body that was used in medieval times
> ঌ The variant spellings of this word include 'pavise' and 'pavisse'.

peag
noun
small shell beads used as jewellery or currency by certain Native American tribes
> ঌ The word is an abbreviation of 'wampumpeag'.

peculation
noun
embezzlement, pilfering or misappropriation of money

pedalfer
noun
a soil rich in alumina and iron but deficient in calcium carbonate and so usually acidic

pellucid
adjective
1 (of water, light, etc) transparent, clear
2 (of speech, sound, etc) absolutely clear
   🙰 The word is derived from Latin *per-* 'through' and *lucere* 'to shine'.

pelong
noun
a satin-like silk fabric

penetrance
noun
(in genetics) the frequency with which the properties controlled by a gene will be expressed in those individuals that possess it; this is usually given as a percentage

pennoncel
noun
a long narrow tapering flag or streamer borne on a lance

periclitate
verb
to expose to danger; to put at risk
   🙰 The word is pronounced 'pe-*rik*-li-tayt', with the stress on the second syllable.

pericope
noun
a short passage or extract from a book, especially one from a religious text that is selected as a reading in public worship

perigee

noun

(in astronomy) the point in the orbit of a body, such as the Moon, when it is closest to the Earth

perioeci

noun

people who live on the same parallel of latitude but on opposite sides of the Earth

&> In ancient Greece, the *perioeci* or *perioikoi* were free men of Sparta who were not citizens of the state and lived in the hills and coastal areas around the city. The word comes from Greek *peri-* 'around' and *oikos* 'dwelling' and is pronounced 'pe-ri-*ee*-sai', with the stress on the third syllable.

peripatetic

adjective

1 travelling from place to place; itinerant
2 (of a teacher) employed by more than one school or college and so obliged to travel between them

&> The word is derived from Greek *peri-* 'around' and *pateein* 'to walk'. The term 'Peripatetic' was used to denote the school of philosophers founded by Aristotle, because of his habit of walking in the Lyceum in Athens while he was teaching.

peripeteia or peripetia

noun

a sudden change of fortune, especially in drama

&> The word is derived from Greek *peri-* 'around' and *piptein* 'to fall'.

peristalith

noun

(in archaeology) a circle of standing stones that encloses a cairn or barrow built over a chamber tomb

&> The word is formed from Greek *peri-* 'around', *histanai* 'to set up' and *lithos* 'stone'.

perite
adjective
skilled

perjink
noun
a fusspot; an 'old maid'
adjective
1 neat; having a smart appearance
2 prim; strait-laced
3 exact; precise; scrupulously careful; fussy; finicking
 ঌ This Scots word is of unknown origin.

perkin
noun
1 a kind of weak cider, especially one made from a second pressing of the apples
2 rough dregs and mulch left from cider-making

perlustrate
verb
1 to travel through an area conducting a thorough inspection or survey
2 to scrutinize documents and correspondence for the purposes of surveillance

peroration
noun
1 the concluding part of a speech or written discourse, summing up the points made in the earlier part
2 a long formal speech

perpending
noun
1 the action of pondering or considering
2 a consideration or reflection

persiflage

noun

banter; teasing or flippant talk

ও The word is derived from French *persifler* 'to banter'.

perspicuous

adjective

(of speech or writing) clearly expressed; easily understood

pervenche

noun

1 the periwinkle

2 a shade of light, reddish blue similar to the colour of periwinkle flowers

phallocrat

noun

a person who assumes or advocates the existence of a male-dominated society, or the superiority of men over women because of their sex

pheon

noun

(in heraldry) a 'broad arrow' device resembling the head of a spear or javelin with smooth blades on the outside and long barbs on the inner edge

philavery

noun

an idiosyncratic collection of uncommon and pleasing words

ও The term 'philavery' was coined by my mother-in-law during a game of Scrabble. While discussing a suitable name for this collection she managed to trump any of my suggestions with this word, loosely constructed from Greek *phileein* 'to love' and Latin *verbum* 'a word'. The recommended pronunciation is 'fil-*a*-vuh-ri', with the stress on the second syllable.

phlogiston

noun

a substance believed in earlier times to exist in all combustible matter and to be released in combustion; the observed effects were subsequently found to be due to oxygen

photism

noun

a hallucinatory vision of a light, often coloured

phrenologist

noun

someone who examines the shape and protuberances of a person's skull to assess their character and aptitudes

phugoid

adjective

(in aeronautics) relating to the longitudinal stability of an aircraft or missile in flight, especially the oscillations in its flight path

physiocrat

noun

a follower of a school of thought originating in 18th-century France which propounded the belief that a country's wealth is derived solely from its agriculture

piblokto

noun

a condition affecting Inuit peoples and Arctic animals in winter, when excitable, hysterical or irrational behaviour is followed by depression or stupor

Pierian

adjective

relating to Pieria, or to the Muses (and hence to poetry and learning)

&ep; Pieria is in a region of Greece close to Mount Olympus, which was regarded as the home of the Muses of Greek and Roman mythology.

piki
noun
a bread made from maize-meal by the Hopi Indians of the south-western USA

piligerous
adjective
covered in hair or down

pinlock
noun
the fee paid to the keeper of a pound for impounding stray livestock

piquer or piqué
verb
to insert garlic, herbs or other flavourings into slits in meat or poultry before cooking, or to lard the meat with bacon etc

pisang
noun
(in Malaysian and Indonesian cuisine) a banana or a plantain
    • The word is pronounced 'pi-*sang*', with the stress on the second syllable.

piskun
noun
a trap for buffalo used by Native Americans

pismo clam
noun
a large edible marine clam, *Tivela stultorum*, found on the southern Pacific coast of North America

pistic
adjective
(possibly) pure; genuine
    • The Greek *nardos pistikos* is translated 'spikenard' in translations of

the Bible; it is not clear whether 'pistic' is a local name or a quality of the ointment.

planxty
noun
(in Irish traditonal music) a melody for the harp

plap
verb
1 to fall or drop with a dull sound
2 to make a light slapping sound
   ﹔ Like 'parp' mentioned above, 'plap' is another one of those endearingly playful, onomatopoeic words which seem to be designed to bring a smile to the face and an image to the mind. *The Chambers Dictionary* describes the term 'plap' as 'a flatter sound than a plop'.

pleionosis
noun
a tendency to exaggerate one's own importance; self-aggrandizement

plenarium
noun
a book containing religious matter of one kind that would otherwise be spread amongst several books, eg the collection of all material relating to the Christian liturgy into a missal or the Book of Common Prayer

plenilunary
adjective
relating to the full moon

pleonasm
noun
1 (in rhetoric) the use of more words than are needed to express something
2 an unnecessary word or words

plochteach
noun
a photosensitivity disease affecting lambs
> The disease is known by a variety of other names, including 'saut' and 'yellowses'. This particular name is borrowed from Gaelic.

pluries
noun
(in law) a writ issued after two earlier writs have been ignored
> The word is Latin, meaning 'many times, often'. It occurred in the first clause of writs when these were written in Latin, and so came to be applied to the writ itself.

plutogogue
noun
someone who speaks on behalf of or whose words are intended to appeal to the wealthy

pluvial
noun
(in geology) a period of extended rainfall
adjective
1 relating to rain; rainy
2 (in geology) caused by rain

podiacide
noun
the act of (metaphorically) shooting oneself in the foot, ie a stupid or irrational act which causes self-inflicted harm to one's image or standing and which could have been prevented or avoided
> The word, a blend of 'podiatry' and 'suicide', was reputedly coined by a US military officer, and became widely known in autumn 2006 when the US ambassador to the United Nations used it to describe a speech by the Venezuelan president that had lost Venezuela its nomination to the Security Council.

podiatrist
noun
a chiropodist
> The word is derived from Greek *pous* 'foot' and *iatros* 'physician'.

pogonophilia
noun
a love of beards

pogonophobia
noun
an irrational fear of beards

pogonotrophy
noun
the cultivation of a beard, moustache or other facial hair

poikilitic
adjective
1 (in geology) denoting a rock or its texture in which large grains or mineral crystals enclose smaller ones
2 (in geology) mottled with various colours
> The word is derived from Greek *poikilos* 'multicoloured, changeable'

polypragmatic
adjective
officious; meddling

prandial
adjective
relating to dinner or lunch
> The word is derived from Latin *prandium*, referring to a morning or midday meal. It is a jocular term, usually used with 'pre-' or 'post-'; hence, 'preprandial', meaning 'before dinner or lunch' and 'postprandial', meaning 'after dinner or lunch'.

prangle
verb
to press together; to pinch

praxis
noun
1 the practical application or exercise of knowledge or a theory
2 established practice; custom

predella
noun
1 the platform or step on which an altar stands, or a raised shelf at the back of an altar
2 (in art) a small painting or sculpture attached to the predella, or a small picture attached a larger one, especially beneath an altarpiece

prelapsarian
adjective
relating to the time before the Fall of Man and the expulsion of Adam and Eve from the Garden of Eden; innocent

prepense
adjective
(especially in law) premeditated, intended

prescience
noun
foreknowledge, foresight

prestidigitation
noun
sleight of hand
> ঌ The word is derived from French *prestidigitateur*, a combination of French *preste* 'nimble' and Latin *digitus* 'finger'.

priapic
adjective
1 relating to or resembling a phallus

2 excessively concerned with masculinity and male sexuality

ॐ The origins of this term lie with Priapus, one of the many fertility gods of classical antiquity, whose worship spread from Asia Minor to Greece and Rome. Believed to originate in phallic images used in the worship of Dionysus, the god of wine, he was generally depicted as an ugly Pan-like figure with enormous genitals. In most accounts he was described as the son of Aphrodite and Dionysus, afflicted with his deformities by the jealous goddess Hera. The patron of crops and flocks, winemaking, beekeeping and gardens, he was represented all over the classical world by phallic statues or 'herms', often painted red, placed in gardens and fields in order to promote fertility.

prink
verb
to dress up; to smarten up; to preen

ॐ The word's origin is unclear but it is probably related to Middle Low German *prank* 'pomp' and Dutch *pronk* 'finery'.

procacity
noun
forwardness; pertness; petulance; impudence

procellous
adjective
stormy; tempestuous

procerity
noun
height; tallness

processualism
noun
(in archaeology) a theory that the cultural evolution of societies can be understood through scientific analysis of artifacts etc

proctalgia
noun
pain in the rectum or at the anus

> ৪▶ The word is derived from Greek *proktos* 'anus' and *algos* 'pain' and is one which I find can be rather useful when describing certain people.

prog
noun
provisions obtained by begging or vagrancy
verb
to obtain food and other provisions by begging, pilfering or scavenging; to forage

prolicide
noun
the crime of killing one's offspring, either in the womb or shortly after birth

prolix
adjective
(of speech or writing) tediously lengthy; verbose
> ৪▶ The word is derived via French from Latin *prolixus* 'poured forth, stretched out'.

propinquity
noun
1 nearness in place or time; proximity
2 close kinship

propylaeum or propylon
noun
(in architecture) a monumental entrance, usually to a temple
> ৪▶ The word is pronounced 'prop-i-*lee*-um', with the stress on the third syllable, and is derived from Greek *pro-* 'before' and *pyle* 'gate'. The most famous example is the Propylaeum at the entrance to the Acropolis in Athens.

prosateur or prosator
noun
a writer of prose

proscenium

noun

1 (in a theatre) the part of the stage in front of the curtain, and the enclosing arch
2 (in the ancient world) the stage of a theatre

} The word is pronounced 'proh-*seen*-i-um', with the stress on the second syllable.

prosopagnosia

noun

an inability to recognize familiar faces, often referred to as 'face blindness'

prosopography

noun

a study of a particular historical or social context through the life, career, connections, etc of an individual or a group

prosopopoeia

noun

1 a figure of speech in which an absent or imaginary person is represented as speaking or acting
2 a figure of speech in which an inanimate or abstract thing is represented in human form or with human attributes

prospicience

noun

foresight; prevision

} The word is pronounced 'pros-*pis*-i-uns', with the stress on the second syllable.

prothonotary

noun

1 the principal clerk or registrar in certain law courts
2 one of the twelve members of the college of Roman Catholic church prelates responsible for the registration of papal acts, recording beatifications, canonizations, etc

prushun
noun
(US slang) a boy who travels with an experienced tramp, begging and stealing for him and also providing sexual gratification

pudent
adjective
experiencing or showing shame

pullulate
verb
1 to abound
2 to develop, spring up
3 to breed prolifically
> ৯ The word is derived from Latin *pullulare* 'to sprout out', from *pullus* 'young animal'.

pullus
noun
a young bird still at the downy stage prior to fledging

pulqueria
noun
(in Mexico) a shop or inn selling *pulque*, an alcoholic beverage made from the fermented sap of agave plants
> ৯ Described as having an 'interesting' taste similar to buttermilk, *pulque* contains around six per cent alcohol and is rich in carbohydrates, amino acids and vitamins. An ancient predecessor of the better-known Mexican exports mescal and tequila, it is depicted in Aztec carvings dating back to around AD 200 and plays an important part in Mesoamerican mythology. The Aztec fertility goddess Mayahuel was the patron of the agave, and mother of the 400 rabbit gods of drunkenness to whom she fed *pulque* via her 400 breasts.

punctiliar
adjective
relating to or occurring at a specific point in time

pungle or pongale
verb
(US slang) to pay (up); to contribute; to put down money

pungy
noun
a type of small schooner used for oyster-fishing and carrying cargo in Chesapeake Bay, USA

pusillanimity
noun
timidness, faint-heartedness
> ও The word is derived from Latin *pusillus* 'very small' and *animus* 'mind'.

pyal
noun
(in southern India) a raised platform running along the front of a house under the verandah on which people sit during the day and sleep in hot weather

pyrophoric
adjective
1 igniting on exposure to air
2 emitting sparks when friction is applied

qi

noun

(in Chinese philosophy) the life force inherent in all things

ʖ▸ This is a variant spelling of 'chi'.

quacksalver

noun

a quack or charlatan

quaestuary

noun

1 someone employed to collect profits
2 someone whose prime concern is financial gain
adjective
seeking to gain

quaintise

noun

1 ingenuity; subtlety; cunning
2 a ploy or stratagem

quandong

noun

the name of a variety of native Australian trees, and the fruit and timber they produce

ʖ▸ The variant spellings of this word include 'quandang' and 'quantong'.

quattie

noun

1 a coin to the value of 1½ pennies that was used in Jamaica when it was a British colony
2 (Jamaican patois) something of no value

querimony

noun

a complaint; complaining

quiddity

noun

1 the essence of something; its distinctive qualities
2 a quibble; a trivial point or objection
ह्ल The word is derived from Latin *quid* 'what'.

quidnunc

noun

a nosy person; a gossipmonger
ह्ल The word is derived from Latin *quid* 'what' and *nunc* 'now'.

quiescent

adjective

1 quiet, silent
2 motionless, inactive

quisquous

adjective

perplexing; debatable; dubious

quodlibet

noun

1 (in philosophy or theology) a topic put forward for discussion
2 a medley of well-known tunes
ह्ल The word derives from Latin *quod* 'what' and *libet* 'it pleases'.

Rr

raceme
noun
(in botany) a flower-head with each flower attached by a short stalk at equal distances along the main stem
ॐ The word is derived from Latin *racemus* 'bunch of grapes'.

rambunctious
adjective
(North American colloquialism) exuberant, boisterous, difficult to control

rampallion
noun
a scoundrel; ruffian; good-for-nothing; wretch

rantipole
noun
a wild, romping young person
adjective
wild; roving; rakish

ranula
noun
a cyst on the underside of the tongue or the floor of the mouth

rappel

noun
the drum beat used to call soldiers to arms
verb
to abseil
    ❧ The word is French, meaning 'recall'.

rath

noun
(in Ireland) an ancient fortified settlement surrounded by a bank of earth

ratiocination

noun
1 the process of reasoning methodically and logically
2 the conclusion or proposition arrived at by this process, especially by the use of syllogisms

rato

abbreviation
rocket-assisted take-off
    ❧ This term is used of the take-off of a jet aircraft when thrust is boosted by a rocket engine.

rebarbative

adjective
repellant
    ❧ The word is derived from French *rébarbatif*, from *barbe* 'beard'.

recalescence

noun
a spontaneous and temporary rise in the temperature of ferrous metal during the process of cooling from white heat

recension

noun
1 a critical revision of a text incorporating the most likely elements of different versions

2 the version of a text revised in this manner

recondite
adjective
difficult to understand; obscure

recrement
noun
waste matter; refuse, dross, scum

refocillation
noun
restoration of strength or vigour through refreshment

reg
noun
a type of desert terrain characterized by rocky and gravelly surfaces

regelation
noun
the process of freezing together again

reification
noun
the process of mentally converting something (an abstraction, a person, etc) into a thing; the representation or expression of an abstraction in material form

remicle
noun
the outermost primary feather in the wings of certain birds
    ❧ This feather is smaller than the other primaries, and evolution seems to have left it without a function.

remiped
noun
an animal with limbs like oars, particularly some crustaceans

adjective
having limbs, especially feet, adapted for use in such a way
𐰁 The word is derived from Latin *remus* 'oar' and *pes* 'foot'.

remontado
noun
someone who returns to the mountains or other wild places and
avoids civilization, either through choice or as a fugitive

remontoir
noun
(in clocks etc) a device that provides a regular energy impulse to a
pendulum or balance; an escapement

repullulate
verb
to bud, sprout or germinate again

resile
verb
1 to draw back from an agreement, contract, course of action, etc
2 to draw back or recoil in aversion
3 to recoil or spring back into a former size, shape, position, etc

resipiscence
noun
recognition of past mistakes and desire to do better in future
𐰁 The word is derived from Latin *resipiscere* which means 'to recover
one's senses', and is a useful term for any member of the business
community to remember.

rhabdomancy
noun
divination using a rod or wand, especially to find water or mineral ore
𐰁 More commonly known as 'rod divining' or 'dowsing', this term is
derived from the Greek words *rhabdos* 'rod' and *manteia* 'divination'.
I gained first-hand experience of this practice some years ago, after I
bought a 17th-century thatched stone cottage in Wiltshire. Although

it had an idyllic setting, there was something unwholesome about the place: we noticed strange smells and we often did not sleep well. Eventually we employed the services of a rhabdomancer. He used both rods and a weight on the end of a line and could, apparently, divine negative energy running through the building. He attempted to counteract these forces by hammering hollow metal tubes into the ground at opposite diagonal corners of the house. Alas, I am not in a position to say whether these had a beneficial effect, as we sold the house before any perceptible change occurred.

rhinal
adjective
relating to the nose
> ⁂ This comes from the Greek word *rhis* 'nostril, nose'.

rhinegrave
noun
1 a German count whose lands bordered the River Rhine
2 a type of very full-skirted men's breeches worn in the 17th century

rhonchisonant
adjective
snorting, or making a snorting noise
> ⁂ The word is pronounced 'rong-*kis*-uh-nunt', with the stress on the second syllable.

ricasso
noun
the unedged section of a sword's blade just above the guard

rictus
noun
1 the expanse or gape of an open mouth or beak
2 an unnatural, fixed grin or grimace

riparian
noun
an owner of land on a river bank

adjective
relating to a river bank; riverine

risible
adjective
1 exciting laughter; laughable; ludicrous
2 given to laughter

risse
noun
a brawl or quarrel

rodomontade
noun
1 a boastful or bragging speech
2 boastful or bragging words or behaviour
    ৡ The word comes from French *rodomont* and Italian *rodomonte*, after
    the boastful king Rodomonte in Ariosto's epic poem *Orlando Furioso*
    (1516).

roil
verb
1 to make a liquid cloudy by agitating it so that dregs, sediment, etc
are stirred up
2 (in USA) to anger; to upset

rongeur
noun
a surgical instrument for removing small pieces of bone

ronion or ronyon
noun
a mangy or scabby creature; a term of contempt for a woman

roodge
verb
1 to push or lift
2 to move with effort

roque
noun
a form of croquet played in the USA, using short-handled mallets and ten hoops on a hard court bounded by a wall against which the ball can rebound and be retrieved

rostrous
adjective
having a beak or snout

rube
noun
a country bumpkin
 ₧ A North American colloquialism, this is derived from the personal name Reuben.

rupestrian
adjective
done on stone or rocks, eg inscriptions, cave paintings

ruptuary
noun
a commoner, someone who is not of noble blood

rutilant
adjective
1 bright red
2 glowing with a ruddy or golden light

ryokan
noun
a traditional Japanese inn
 ₧ The ryokan, whose origins date back to the Nara period of 710–784, embodies the unique spirit of traditional Japanese hospitality. Usually traditionally built and found in secluded and rural areas, ryokans offer guests the opportunity to experience at first hand ancient Japanese customs and traditions; loved by Japanese people they are becoming increasingly popular with foreign tourists.

Ss

sabretache

noun

a flat leather satchel suspended by long straps from the left side of the sword-belt of a cavalry officer

    👄 The word is pronounced '*sab*-uh-tash', with the stress on the first syllable.

sachem

noun

leader

    👄 An Algonquian word originally applied to the supreme chief of some Native American tribes, in more recent times the word has become a North American colloquialism for a political leader.

sackbut

noun

an early wind instrument similar to a trombone

    👄 The word is derived from French *saquer* 'to pull' and *bouter* 'to push'.

sagamore

noun

a Native American chief

    👄 The word is derived from the Penobscot word *sagamo*.

salient

noun

1 a projecting angle of a fortification

2 an outward bulge in a line of troops
adjective
1 standing out; prominent; conspicuous; (of an angle) pointing outwards
2 (of a heraldic animal) standing on its hind legs with its front legs raised
3 leaping, dancing, spouting forth

samizdat

noun
1 (in the former Communist countries of eastern Europe) the clandestine copying and distribution of writings banned by the government
2 the writings themselves

> ࣷ The word is derived from Russian, meaning 'self-published'.

sapid

adjective
1 having flavour, especially a pleasant flavour
2 having intellectual interest; not dull

sarcology

noun
the branch of anatomy that deals with the soft, fleshy parts of the body, eg internal organs, muscles, nerves, blood, etc

satyriasis

noun
excessive or uncontrollable sexual desire in men

> ࣷ The male equivalent of nymphomania, the condition is named after the satyr of Greek mythology, a creature half-man and half-horse or goat. It is pronounced 'sat-i-*rai*-uh-sis', with the stress on the third syllable.

sawder

noun
flattery; exaggerated and ingratiating praise

> ࣷ This is a variant spelling of 'solder', used in the phrase 'soft solder', meaning 'soft soap'.

saxificous
adjective
having the property of turning things to stone
> ॐ This neologism appears in the fantastical 1904 novel *Hadrian the Seventh* by Frederick Rolfe, the English novelist and eccentric whose pseudonyms included amongst others, 'A Crab Maid' and 'Baron Corvo'.

scabrous
adjective
1 (of skin) rough and flaky or scaly; scurfy; bristly
2 (of a subject, situation, etc) difficult to handle
3 indecent, bawdy, salacious

scad
noun
any fish of the Carangidae family, which usually have elongated bodies with large spiky scales, and especially the horse mackerel
> ॐ The word is believed to be derived from Cornish dialect.

scatology
noun
1 (in medicine, palaeontology, etc) the study of excrement or dung
2 a morbid interest in excrement or excretory functions
3 obscene language or literature, especially that concerned with excrement or excretory functions
> ॐ The word is derived from Greek *skatos* 'dung' and *logos* 'study'.

schizzo or skizzo
noun
a sketch

sciatherical or sciotherical
adjective
1 relating to the recording of the shadows cast by heavenly bodies, especially the Sun, as a means of determining the time
2 relating to a sundial
> ॐ The word is pronounced 'sai-uh-*the*-ri-kul', rhyming with 'hysterical'.

sciolism

noun

superficial pretensions to knowledge

> ৯৯ The word is pronounced '*sai*-uh-lizm', with the stress on the first syllable.

scoad

verb

(in south-west English dialect) to scatter, especially a top dressing on agricultural land

scopology

noun

a name suggested in the 18th century for the study of the 'ends' or purposes of human conduct

scordatura

noun

a method of tuning string instruments that produces a different effect to the normal method of tuning

scow

noun

a flat-bottomed boat used for transporting freight

> ৯৯ The word is derived from Dutch *schouw* 'ferry boat'.

scriptorium

noun

a room set apart for writing, especially in a monastery

scumble

verb

to soften the effect of a drawing or painting by applying a very thin coat of opaque or semi-opaque colour, by light rubbing or by applying paint with a dry brush

noun

1 the effect produced by this technique
2 the material used to achieve this effect

scunner
noun
1 a strong dislike; an aversion
2 an object of disgust or loathing
verb
to feel disgust or nausea

seavy
adjective
overgrown with rushes
› In northern English dialect, 'seave' means 'a rush'.

seely court
noun
a fairy court or entourage
› 'Seely' means 'happy' or 'auspicious'.

selenodesy
noun
the branch of mathematics that calculates the shape, size, etc of the Moon or large areas of it
› The word is derived from Greek *selene* 'Moon' and *daisis* 'division'. It is pronounced 'sel-ee-*nod*-i-si', rhyming with 'odyssey'.

semiology
noun
the study of signs and symbols, and how meaning is made and understood
› The novelist and semiotician Umberto Eco has perhaps done more than any other modern thinker to bring the concept of semiology to popular attention in recent years.

seneschal
noun
1 (in the Middle Ages) the steward in charge of the household or estate of a lord or prince
2 the title of a judge on the island of Sark in the Channel Islands
› The word is derived via French and Latin from Germanic words meaning 'old' and 'servant'.

sequitur
noun
a conclusion that follows from the premises or evidence
> ౼ The word is Latin, meaning 'it follows'. This is, of course, the opposite of a 'non sequitur'.

sessle
verb
(in southern English dialects) to fidget; to move about restlessly

se-tenant
noun
(in philately) two or more postage stamps printed together on the same sheet but differing in design or value

shallop
noun
1 a small open boat with oars or sails, or both, which is used in shallow water
2 a large heavy boat, usually two-masted and fore-and-aft-rigged
> ౼ The word is derived from French *chaloupe*, either from Dutch *sloep* 'sloop', or from the obsolete French *chaloppe* 'nutshell'.

shill
noun
(North American slang) someone who acts as an enthusiastic customer or gambler to lure others to buy, gamble, etc

shiur
noun
a lecture or period of study of Jewish religious texts

shonky
adjective
1 underhand, illicit
2 unreliable or inferior
> ౼ The word is mainly used in informal Australian English.

shott
noun
a salt marsh or lake, especially in North Africa, which is usually dry in summer but may contain water in winter
ঌ The word is derived from an Arabic word meaning 'bank, coast'. It is also spelt 'chott'.

shouse
noun
(Australian slang) a toilet, usually outside the house
ঌ The word is pronounced so as to rhyme with 'mouse'.

siagonology
noun
the study of jaw-bones

sialogogue
noun
a medicine that stimulates the secretion of saliva

sibilant
noun
a letter or letters pronounced with a hiss, eg 's', 'sh'
adjective
having a hissing sound

sibylline
adjective
1 prophetic; oracular
2 cryptic
ঌ The word is derived from 'sibyl', meaning a seeress who uttered oracles and prophecies under divine influence at one of the shrines of ancient Greece and Rome; their sayings were often ambiguous, hence the second sense of the word.

sicarian
noun
a murderer; an assassin

„ The Romans used the term *sicarii* of the Jewish zealots who fought a guerrilla war against the Roman occupation of Palestine in the 1st century AD.

sideration

noun

the condition of being affected by the influence of the planets

„ This term, stemming from the Latin *sidus*, 'a star', is usually used of blast in plants or a sudden, apparently inexplicable, affliction with disease.

sitophobia

noun

an abnormal fear of food and eating

„ The word is pronounced 'sai-toh-*foh*-bi-uh', with the stress on the third syllable.

sivet

noun

a tongueless buckle on a saddle from which hang stirrup leathers or girth straps

sixte

noun

a position in fencing

skerrick

noun

(usually with a negative) a very small quantity, a scrap

„ This colloquialism is common to the USA, New Zealand and, especially, Australia. Its origin is unknown but it is believed to be derived from a northern English dialect.

skirling

noun

1 a shrill sound, such as that made by bagpipes
2 a small trout or salmon

slangam

noun
(derogatory) a tall, lanky person

slubberdegullion

noun
a mean, slovenly oaf

smell-smock

noun
a licentious man; a womanizer

• This is also the English dialect name of a number of wild flowers, including the wood anemone, the cuckoo flower or lady's smock, and the wood sorrel.

smew

noun
a small duck, *Mergus albellus*, found in northern Europe and Asia

sniddle

noun
1 coarse grass, rushes or sedge
2 stubble

• This is a dialect word from north-west England.

sobornost

noun
the unity of believers participating freely in a loving fellowship without excessive individualism or the imposition of unity by an external authority

sobriquet or soubriquet

noun
a nickname; an assumed name

• The word is French, meaning originally 'chuck under the chin'.

soffit

noun

(in architecture) a term applied variously to the underside of an arch, balcony, eaves, top of a window or door opening, stair, etc

soi-disant

adjective

so-styled; pretended; would-be

෨ This is French, meaning 'calling oneself'.

Solander box

noun

a wooden box used for storing books, prints, etc, whose lid and base both have three sides of roughly the same height and a fourth side that acts as a hinge. When closed, the sides of the base nest within those of the lid

෨ This type of box is named after the botanist Daniel Solander, who invented it while working at the British Museum in the late 18th century.

solenoglyph

adjective

denoting a group of snakes that possess long, articulated erectile fangs that can inject venom deeply, eg the vipers and adders

sophomania

noun

the delusion that one possesses superior intelligence or wisdom

sophomoric

adjective

relating to a second-year student at university or high school in the USA

෨ The word is derived from Greek *sophos* 'wise' and *moros* 'foolish'.

sorbite

noun

1 a sugar-like substance that occurs naturally in the ripe berries of

the service tree and the rowan and is extracted as a white crystalline substance or syrup
2 the structure of steel resulting from the tempering of martensite

soterial
adjective
(in Christian theology) relating to soteriology, ie the doctrine of salvation
    ♘ The word is derived from Greek *soteria* 'salvation', from *soter* 'saviour'.

souper
noun
(in 19th-century Ireland) a Protestant who supplied famine relief, usually soup, to starving Roman Catholics provided they renounced Catholicism

spanandry
noun
(in zoology) a lack of males or very low ratio of males to females in a population

sparadrap
noun
1 a cloth coated in ointment etc and used as a bandage
2 an adhesive plaster
    ♘ Originally the word referred to a waterproof waxed cloth used for wrapping a dead body.

spavin
noun
1 a disease of the lower leg in horses
2 a hard bony swelling symptomic of this disease

sperage
noun
asparagus

sphragistics
noun
the study of seals and signet rings
> 👁 The word is derived from Greek *sphragis* 'seal'.

spica
noun
1 (in botany) a flower spike or other plant part that resembles a spike
2 (in medicine) a spiral bandage wrapped in a series of reverse turns, so that it resembles an ear of barley

splanchnic
adjective
(in anatomy) relating or belonging to the viscera; intestinal
> 👁 The word is derived via Latin from Greek *splagchna* 'entrails'.

splendacious
adjective
very splendid

spleuchan
noun
a pouch, usually made of leather, for holding tobacco or money

spraints
noun
otter droppings
> 👁 The quirky origins of this unusual term lie in the Old French word *espraintes*, which literally means 'squeezed out'. Other illuminating alternatives to 'dung' or 'droppings' include 'fumet' (deer), 'crottels' (hares), 'scumber' (dogs, foxes) and the more familiar 'guano' (seabirds).

Staunton
adjective
relating to the standard design of chess pieces
> 👁 This design is named after the 19th-century British polymath and chess master Howard Staunton.

stegophily
noun
the practice of climbing the outside of buildings and other structures for sport
> ༆ The pastime is more commonly known as 'buildering', 'urban climbing' or 'structuring'.

stercoraceous
adjective
consisting of or relating to faeces
> ༆ The word is derived from Latin *stercus* 'dung'.

stertorous
adjective
(of breathing) noisy; sounding like snoring

stillatory
noun
1 a still; an apparatus used for distilling
2 a place in which distillation is carried out; a laboratory; a still room

stochastic
adjective
1 (in statistics) random; governed by the laws of probability
2 conjectural

stoush
noun
(Australian and New Zealand slang) fighting; a brawl or fight; a scrap

stramineous
adjective
1 consisting of straw; resembling straw or its colour
2 without value

strumple
noun
the fleshy stem of a horse's tail

stupa
noun
a round, dome-roofed monument used to house Buddhist relics or commemorate significant aspects of Buddhism or Jainism
> ও The word is derived from Sanskrit *stupah* 'tuft of hair, crown of the head, summit'.

suaviate
verb
to kiss

subfusc
noun
dark clothing worn for certain formal occasions at Oxford and Cambridge universities
adjective
dusky, gloomy, sombre
> ও The word is derived from Latin *sub-* 'close to, towards' and *fuscus* 'dark brown'.

succedaneum
noun
(in medicine) a medicine or drug that can act as a substitute for another

succussion
noun
vigorous shaking, especially as a means of detecting whether fluid or air is present in a body cavity

suggillate
verb
to beat severely, until black and blue

sunyata
noun
(in Buddhism) the concept of the emptiness and impermanence of all things

ह‌ This is a Sanskrit word meaning 'emptiness, non-existence'.

supererogation
noun
1 doing more than duty or circumstances require
2 superfluous

ह‌ The word is derived from Latin *super-* 'above, beyond' and *erogare* 'to pay out'. It is pronounced 'soo-puh-re-ruh-*gay*-shun', with the stress on the fifth syllable.

supernaculum
noun
the finest wine, which is so good it is drunk to the last drop
adverb
entirely

ह‌ The word is Latin for 'upon the nail', referring to a custom of turning over a drained glass and letting the last drop of wine fall onto the thumbnail.

surrepent
adjective
creeping beneath or stealthily; stealing upon someone

susurration
noun
a whispering, rustling or murmuring sound

swad
noun
1 a bunch, collection, group
2 (in Scots and English dialect) a soldier

sward
noun
1 a large area of short grass
2 turf

ह‌ The word is derived from Old English *sweard* 'skin'.

swaver
verb
1 to totter; to sway about; to move unsteadily
2 to hesitate; to dither

swikedom
noun
treachery; betrayal; deceit

syllogism
noun
1 a form of reasoning in which a conclusion is drawn from two statements; a common term is present in both statements but not in the conclusion, which may be valid or invalid
2 deductive reasoning from general rather than particular cases

sylvan
adjective
relating to woods or woodland; wooded; romantically rural, arcadian
noun
a wood-god, a forest-dweller

&⤳ A wonderfully aesthetic term which originates in the Latin *silva*, meaning 'wood'.

synaesthesia
noun
a sensation produced in one part of the body or one sense when another part or sense is stimulated

synastry
noun
a concurrence of the positions of the planets, stars, etc, which in astrology indicates the similarity of the fortunes of two people

syncretism
noun
(in philosophy and theology) the attempted merging or reconciliation of differing philosophies or religions

• The word is derived from Greek *synkretismos* 'a confederation', and originally referred to a union of Cretans against a common enemy.

synecdoche

noun

a figure of speech in which a part is used to represent the whole, the specific for the general, etc, and vice versa

• The word is pronounced 'sin-*ek*-duh-kee', with the stress on the second syllable.

synezesis or synizesis

noun

the union of two adjacent vowels or a vowel and a diphthong in pronunciation to contract two successive syllables into one

syzygy

noun

1 (in astronomy) the alignment of three celestial bodies, especially the Sun, the Earth and the Moon, along a straight or nearly straight line
2 any pair of connected or co-related things

• This delightful word is pronounced '*siz*-i-ji', with the stress on the first syllable. It is derived via Latin from the Greek word *syzygia*, meaning 'union' from *syn-* 'together, like' and *zygon* 'yoke'. It is also the very clever and apt name of one of my favourite restaurants, in Aspen, Colorado.

Tt

taft

noun

a widening-out at the end of a lead pipe that forms a broad thin flange

taggeen

noun

a small glass of spirits; a dram

tammar

noun

a small scrub wallaby, *Macropus eugenii*, found on islands off the south-western coast of Australia (but now extinct on the mainland) and in New Zealand

tantivy

noun

a fast gallop

adverb

at full gallop; headlong

> The word came to be used in the 17th century of the sound of galloping feet, and in the 18th century to refer to a blast on a horn, possibly because of the association with galloping horses of the use of a post-horn or hunting horn.

taphephobia

noun

an abnormal fear of being buried alive

   ॐ The word is derived from Greek *taphos* 'grave' and *phobos* 'fear'.

tapinosis

noun

(in rhetoric) the use of a word or name for something that diminishes it; meiosis

tappen

noun

a 'rectal plug' or indigestible mass in the intestine of hibernating animals that makes defecation difficult during hibernation

tappet

noun

a projecting arm or other part of a machine which moves or is moved by contact with another component

Tarbuck knot

noun

(in mountaineering) a type of non-jamming slip knot which is particularly good at withstanding sudden or heavy strain

tars

noun

a rich, probably silk, fabric originating in central Asia or the Middle East and used in medieval times; also known as cloth of tars

tarsalgia

noun

a general pain in the foot

tarsorrhaphy

noun

an operation to stitch together all or part of the opening between the eyelids

tartine
noun
a slice of bread spread with butter, jam or some other topping

taupie or tawpie
noun
a scatterbrained, untidy, awkward or careless young person, especially a woman

teart
noun
1 soil or plants that contain unusually high levels of molybdenum
2 the diarrhoea suffered by cattle that graze on teart plants
adjective
sour

> ঔ The word is pronounced as two syllables, with the stress on the first: '*tee*-ut'.

teem
verb
1 to be abundant, plentiful
2 to abound in, be full of
3 to pour down; to pour out

> ঔ In senses 1 and 2, the word derives from Old English *teman* 'to give birth'; in sense 3, the word derives from Old English *temen*, from Old Norse *toema* 'to empty'.

telearch
noun
(in ancient Greece) the title of a magistrate in Thebes

teleferic
noun
a cable railway

teleology
noun
the study of design and purpose in events, natural phenomena,

etc, and the use of design and purpose to explain those events, phenomena, etc

teleostean
adjective
relating to fish of the subclass Teleostei, which includes nearly all types of extant fish

tellurian
noun
an inhabitant of the earth
> ꝭ The word is derived from Latin *tellus* 'earth'.

telmatology
noun
the study of wetlands, especially peat-bogs

tembo
noun
(in sub-Saharan Africa) an alcoholic drink made from the sap of various palm trees; palm wine

tenebrific
adjective
1 dark, gloomy
2 darkening; obscuring

tenesmus
noun
(in medicine) a continual need to relieve the bowels or bladder, accompanied by painful but ineffectual straining

tercel or tiercel
noun
a male hawk
> ꝭ The word is derived from Latin *tertius* 'third', possibly because the male is smaller than the female.

tergant
adjective
(in heraldry) showing the back part

tergiversate
verb
1 to equivocate
2 to change one's beliefs or allegiances
> ₯ The word is derived from Latin *tergum* 'back' and *vertere* 'to turn'.

termagant
noun
an overbearing, quarrelsome, shrewish woman; a virago
> ₯ The word is derived from the Termagant, an imaginary deity with a
> violent, scolding character, in medieval morality plays.

testor
noun
1 a witness
2 a person who makes a will

tettix
noun
1 the cicada
2 a genus of small grasshoppers

tewtaw
verb
to beat; to break up fibres by beating
> ₯ The word is derived from 'taw', a word found in Scots and English
> dialects. The noun 'taw' means 'a fibre or fibrous roots of a plant' and
> the verb 'taw' means 'to soften hides by beating; to tease out, comb out
> flax fibres'; 'tew' is an irregular variant of 'taw'.

thaumaturgy
noun
the working of wonders, miracles or magic
> ₯ The word is derived from Greek *thaumos* 'marvel' and *ergon* 'work'.

theandric
adjective
relating to or arising from the union of the divine and human natures in Christ

thersitical
adjective
caustic; abusive in speech; scurrilous; intentionally tactless
> ह्ल्ऌ The word derives from Thersites, an ill-favoured character in Homer's *Iliad*.

thigger or thiggar
noun
a beggar; someone who solicits from other people subsistence, alms or gifts

thigmophilic
adjective
touch-loving; liking or needing to be touched or to feel the touch of something

thiller or thill-horse
noun
a horse that is put between the shafts of a cart or carriage and supports them; the last horse in a team

thoan
adjective
relating to animals of the subgenus *Thous*, which includes certain types of wild dog and jackal

thole
verb
(in Scots and some English dialects) to undergo, suffer, endure
> ह्ल्ऌ The word is derived from Old English *tholian* 'to suffer'.

tholoid
noun
a steep-sided dome of hardened lava that plugs the vent of a volcano

threnody
noun
a lamentation, in song or verse form, especially on someone's death
    ॐ The word is derived from Greek *threnos* 'wailing' and *oide* 'song'.

thumber
noun
someone thumbing a lift; a hitch-hiker

thuringer
noun
(in USA) a summer sausage; a type of sausage that is made in autumn or winter and kept until summer

Tickney
adjective
relating to a coarse type of earthenware produced at Ticknal, near Derby
    ॐ Itinerant sellers of this earthenware were known as 'Tickney men' or 'Tickney women'.

tiggy
noun
1 (British dialect) a hedgehog
2 (in Scots and northern English dialects) the children's game 'tig', or the person who is 'it' in the game
    ॐ Sense 1 is possibly derived from *tig* 'little pig'. Sense 2 might be derived from the Dutch *tikken* 'to pat' or Norwegian *tikke* 'to touch lightly'.

tirshatha
noun
the title of an ancient Persian civil official of high status, possibly equivalent to a viceroy or governor

tomentose or tomentous
adjective
covered in densely matted short woolly hairs or down
  ৡ➤ The word is derived from Latin *tomentum* 'cushion stuffing'.

tonitruous or tonitrous
adjective
thundery; thundering

toot
noun
1 a short, sharp blast of a horn, trumpet, whistle, etc
2 a quantity of a drug, especially cocaine, inhaled through the nose

tope
noun
a small shark
verb
to drink alcohol to excess

topology
noun
1 the study of the topography of a particular place or region, especially with reference to its historical development
2 (in medicine) the study of the anatomical structure of a specific part of the body
3 (in mathematics) the study of the properties of geometrical figures that are unaffected by changes in the size or shape of the figure
4 (in computing) the configuration of the nodes in a local area network
  ৡ➤ The word is derived via German *Topologie* from Greek *topos* 'place' and *logos* 'study'.

toponym
noun
1 a place name
2 a descriptive place name, often taken from a topographical feature of the place

ॐ The word is derived from Greek *topos* 'place' and *onyma* 'name'.

torba

noun
1 (in Malta) a cement-like material made from crushed limestone and pottery shards and traditionally used for the floors of buildings
2 a Turkomen woven bag which is hung up inside a tent to provide storage space

torpillage

noun
electric shock therapy used as a treatment for neurosis, especially in treatment for shell shock during the First World War

torple or torfle

verb
(of an animal) to die

> ॐ A northern English dialect word, it possibly is derived from Middle English *torfie* 'to fall into a decline'.

tourney

noun
a medieval tournament
verb
to take part in a tournament

traduce

verb
1 to malign someone or something in speech or writing
2 to misrepresent someone or something

> ॐ The word is derived from Latin *traducere* 'to disgrace', from *trans-* 'across, beyond' and *ducere* 'to lead'.

treche

verb
to deceive; to cheat

tregetour
noun
a magician or juggler who creates illusions by legerdemain
> ࢞ The word is pronounced '*trej*-uh-tuh', with the stress on the first syllable.

tresaiel
noun
a great-great-grandfather

trewerne
noun
a type of wagon or truck

tribadism
noun
a form of lesbian lovemaking that simulates heterosexual intercourse

trilapse or trelapse
adjective
lapsing for the third time into a sin or offence

trillium
noun
any of several plants of the lily family native to North America and Asia which have a single flower with three petals above a whorl of three leaves

triskaidekaphobia
noun
an abnormal fear of the number thirteen

tristubh
noun
a metre of 11 syllables in Vedic poetry such as the Bhagavad Gita, or any hymn composed in this metre
> ࢞ The word is pronounced '*trish*-tuub', with the stress on the first syllable.

trochoid
noun
1 (in geometry) the curve that a point on the radius of a circle
describes as it rolls along a straight line or along another circle
2 (in anatomy) a bone in a pivot joint that articulates with another
bone with a rotary motion
> ह The word is derived from Greek *trochoeides* 'circular', from *trochos*
> 'wheel'.

troilist
noun
the third person in a *ménage á trois* or sexual encounter involving
three people

troker or truker
noun
a dishonest or disreputable person; a rogue; a cheat

trope
noun
a word or expression used figuratively rather than in its literal
meaning
> ह The word is derived from Greek *tropos* 'a turn'.

trunnion
noun
1 one of the projections on either side of a cannon or mortar that
support it on its carriage and form the axis on which it pivots
2 a hollow gudgeon supporting an oscillating cylinder and conveying
steam in a steam locomotive engine

tsia
noun
tea
> ह This Mandarin Chinese word for tea was one of the names initially
> used in Britain after the beverage was introduced.

tunket
noun
(US euphemism) hell

turdiform
adjective
resembling a thrush
> It is rather unfortunate that such an attractive little bird was given the genus name *Turdus* – misleadingly similar, but quite unrelated to, the Old English-derived 'turd'.

tutelary or tutelar
adjective
1 having the role or authority of a guardian
2 of or relating to a guardian
3 (of supernatural beings) giving protection, especially to a particular person, thing or place

twattle
verb
1 to prattle, chatter idly
2 to pet (an animal)
> This word is an alteration of 'tattle' and subsequently became 'twaddle'.

twire
noun
1 to peer, peep, look covertly
2 (of a light) to twinkle, glance

twofer
noun
(informal) an offer of two items for the price of one

Uu

ubiation

noun

the act of occupying a new place

ultracrepidarian

adjective

expressing opinions on matters beyond one's knowledge; ignorant and presumptuous

&❧ This word derives from a story attributed by Pliny the Elder to the renowned classical Greek artist Apelles. According to Pliny, the artist once heeded the criticism of a cobbler who found fault with a sandal in one of his paintings. When the cobbler then went on to find fault with the subject's leg, however, Apelles is purported to have said *ne sutor ultra crepidam*, 'the cobbler must not go beyond the sandal'.

ultrafidian

adjective

going beyond faith; credulous

ultroneous

adjective

spontaneous; voluntary; of one's own accord

umbel

noun

(in botany) a flower-head in which a cluster of flowers on stalks of nearly equal length spring from the same centre on the main stem, forming a flat or curved surface

 ‽ The word is derived from Latin *umbella* 'sunshade', a diminutive of *umbra* 'shade'.

umbles

plural noun

the edible entrails and internal organs of an animal, especially a deer

 ‽ The 'humble' in the phrase 'humble pie' is a corruption of 'umbles', as these parts of the deer were served to the huntsman, who was of a low social level, while his master enjoyed the better cuts of venison.

umbo

noun

1 the boss on a shield, usually in on near the centre and often having a sharp point
2 (in zoology and botany) a knob or protuberance on the surface of an organism

umbratile

adjective

1 staying or living in the shade or indoors; secluded; retired; reclusive
2 shadowy; unreal; shady

umbration

noun

1 (in heraldry) a charge that is painted in outline only
2 a faint representation; a shadowy indication

umset

verb

to surround; to lay siege to

umyak or umiak

noun

an Inuit boat made from skins stretched over a wooden or bone frame and usually propelled with oars

 ‽ The word means 'woman's boat'; 'kayak' means 'man's boat'.

unalist
noun
a priest or other ecclesiastic who holds only one benefice

unasinous
adjective
being equal in stupidity

unct
verb
to anoint

undergrope
verb
to delve into; to learn; to understand

undinism
noun
(in psychology) a strong, usually sexual, interest in water and urination

ungulate
noun
a hoofed mammal
adjective
1 (in zoology) having the form or shape of a hoof
2 (of mammals) hoofed

unireme
noun
(in the ancient world) a galley with one bank of oars

unnun
verb
to expel a nun from the religious order to which she belongs
   ‽ The word is pronounced 'un-*nun*', with the stress on the second syllable.

unsad
adjective
unreliable; unsteady; fickle

unwrast or unwraste
adjective
1 wretched; worthless; in a poor condition
2 wicked
3 unreliable

uropygium
noun
the rump of a bird, ie the part that supports the tail feathers

urticant
adjective
causing itching or stinging

uxorilocal
adjective
relating to residence after marriage at the home or in the community of the wife

uxorious
adjective
greatly, excessively or submissively fond of one's wife

vagarious
adjective
given to vagaries; capricious; unpredictable; erratic

vagility
noun
(in biology) the ability or tendency of organisms to disperse in a given environment

valeta or veleta
noun
a ballroom dance for couples with a fast waltz-like rhythm, dating from 1900

valetudinarian
noun
a person in poor health; a hypochondriac
adjective
1 relating to or suffering from poor health
2 anxious about one's health; hypochondriac

valonia
noun
the dried acorn cups of evergreen Mediterranean oaks, used in tanning, dyeing and making ink
&ve; The word is derived via Italian *vallonia* from Greek *balanos* 'acorn'.

vapulation
noun
the act of beating or whipping

varlet
noun
1 a menial servant
2 a rascal or rogue
  > Shakespeare is credited with the coinage of the term 'varletry', meaning 'a crowd, a rabble'.

vavasour
noun
(in feudal times) a knight, noble, etc with vassels under him who is himself the vassel of a greater noble

venditate
verb
to blazon; to talk up, as if for sale

vendue
noun
a public auction

veneficial or venefical
adjective
1 acting by poison
2 used in poisoning or in sorcery

venery
noun
1 the hunting of game animals; the chase
2 pursuit of or indulgence in sexual pleasure

vengesour
noun
an avenger

venial
adjective
(of a sin or fault) pardonable, excusable

ventifact
noun
a rock or stone that has been abraded, grooved or polished by wind-borne sand particles

ventoseness
noun
the condition of flatulence, or a tendency to flatulence

veratrine
noun
a poisonous compound obtained from the seeds of the sabadilla and formerly used to treat neuralgia and rheumatism
&ped; The word is derived via French from Latin *veratrum* 'hellebore'.

verdigris
noun
1 a bluish-green coating that forms naturally on copper, brass and bronze surfaces when exposed to air and moisture for long periods, or is created artificially by the action of acetic acid on copper
2 this substance used as a medicine or pigment
&ped; The word is derived from French *vert de Grece* 'green of Greece'.

veridical
adjective
1 truthful; veracious
2 (in psychology) corresponding with what has occurred or occurs subsequently
&ped; The word is derived from Latin *verus* 'true' and *dicere* 'to say'.

vermian
adjective
relating to worms; worm-like

lllll

vermiculate or vermiculated
adjective
1 (in architecture) decorated with shallow wavy lines like worm tracks
2 worm-eaten

verrucose or verrucous
adjective
warty

vespiary
noun
a nest of wasps

vespillo or vespillon
noun
(in ancient Rome) someone who carried out dead bodies at night for burial

vew
noun
(in northern English dialect) a yew tree, or wood obtained from it

vexillation
noun
(in ancient Rome) a body of soldiers grouped under one *vexillum*, or military standard

vexillology
noun
the study of flags

vibrissa
noun
1 a sensitive, bristle-like hair on the face of some animals, eg a cat's whiskers
2 a bristle-like feather by the beak of insect-eating birds
   ≥ The word is derived from Latin *vibrare* 'to shake, swing'.

villeggiatura

noun

a period of residence in the country, usually in the summer to escape the heat of the city

virago

noun

1 a fierce or abusive woman

2 a woman with masculine strength or heroic qualities; an amazon

 ɵ» Many readers will be familiar with the respected international publishing house Virago, which specializes in literature by and for women. The imprint was perhaps named with an element of 'tongue in cheek' considering the most modern definitions of 'virago' as a violent or bad-tempered woman. No doubt there was also a proud acknowledgement of the word's origins, however, of a strong and vigorous woman who raised herself above her modest station. The roots of 'virago', in common with 'virile', 'virtue' and 'hero', lie in the Latin *vir* meaning 'a man'. It appears in the vulgate rendering of Genesis 2.23 as the name Adam gives to Eve, which also sheds light on the publishing house's choice of colophon – a bitten apple.

viscerotonic

adjective

denoting a type of personality that is sociable, easy-going and comfort-loving

 ɵ» This type of personality was associated by the US psychologist William Sheldon with the endomorph body type, ie a soft, round build with a high proportion of fat tissue.

viscus

noun

any of the body's soft internal organs

vitelline

adjective

1 relating to the yolk of an egg

2 resembling the colour of an egg yolk

viviparous
adjective
1 (in zoology) giving birth to live young that have developed within the mother's body
2 (in botany) developing bulbs, seeds or new plants on the parent plant while still attached to it

> ఴ The word is derived from Latin *vivus* 'alive' and *parere* 'to produce'. It is pronounced 'vai-*vip*-uh-rus', with the stress on the second syllable.

vomitory
noun
1 (in architecture) the entrance and exit passages in an amphitheatre or stadium
2 (in medicine) an opening through which matter is discharged
3 an emetic
adjective
causing vomiting

vorage
noun
1 a whirlpool or chasm
2 the act of foraging on the Internet for good video clips to share with others

voussoir
noun
(in architecture) one of the wedge-shaped stones forming an arch; also called an arch stone
verb
to form an arch with voussoirs

wamble

verb

1 to move unsteadily, to stagger

2 (of the stomach) to churn queasily

warby

adjective

(Australian slang) shabby; decrepit; unprepossessing; disreputable

warrok

verb

1 to do up a horse's girth; to bind a person

2 (in Northumbrian dialect) to fasten or tighten the chains or ropes around something

wayzgoose

noun

an annual outing and dinner of the staff of a printing works or the printers of a newspaper

    ⤷ Originally the word applied to a dinner given by a master printer for his workmen each year on or around St Bartholomew's Day (24th August).

wedbedrip

noun

a kind of bedrip, ie a service under which a tenant was bound to provide his feudal lord, on request, with a day's work at harvest-time

whangdoodle
noun
an imaginary creature which features in North American folklore and one of Roald Dahl's children's books

whangee
noun
1 any of several grasses related to bamboo and native to China and Japan
2 a cane made from the stem of the plant
> ॐ The origin is not certain, but is probably derived from Chinese *huang* 'yellow' and *li* 'bamboo'.

wherrit or wherret
verb
to pester, bother or tease

whilom
adjective
former; having once been
> ॐ The word is pronounced '*wai*-lum', with the stress on the first syllable.

whimling
noun
1 someone given to whims
2 a weak, childish person

wimple
noun
a headdress or veil covering the head, the sides of the face and the neck
verb
to wrap in or hide with a wimple; to arrange in folds
> ॐ The word is derived from Old English *wimpel* 'neck-covering'. Worn originally in medieval times as a woman's fashion, the wimple is still part of the dress of some orders of nuns.

witzchoura
noun
a style of long, fur-trimmed lady's mantle with wide, open sleeves fashionable in the early 19th century.

wormling
noun
a little worm

wow-wow or wou-wou
noun
the silvery gibbon, a now endangered species native to Java

> Evocatively named after the sound of its cry, the wow-wow is one of many animals and plants whose name originates in this way. Other delightfully titled creatures include the kittiwake, the chiffchaff, the chickadee, the gecko and the chincherinchee, a South African plant said to be named after the sound its flower stalks make when they move in the wind.

X x

xanthopsia

noun

(in medicine) a condition affecting the eyes that makes objects appear to be yellow or tinged with yellow

→ The word is derived from Greek *xanthos* 'yellow' and *opsis* 'sight'.

xenodochium or xenodochion

noun

1 (in ancient Greece and Rome) a building used to accommodate strangers
2 (in medieval times) a hostel for pilgrims etc, especially in a monastery

xenogenous

adjective

originating outside the organism; caused by a foreign body

xenoglossia

noun

the spontaneous use of a foreign language that the user has not heard before or learned

→ The word is a modern coinage, derived from Greek *xenos* 'strange, foreign' and *glossa* 'tongue'.

yaffle

verb
to eat and drink, especially noisily and greedily
noun
the green woodpecker

yarage

noun
a ship's manoeuvrability and responsiveness at sea

yarborough

noun
a bridge or whist hand that contains no cards higher than a nine
  ❧ This type of hand is named after the 2nd Earl of Yarborough, who is said to have bet odds of 1,000 to 1 against such a hand occurring.

yarwhelp

noun
a common name for the European bar-tailed godwit and the black-tailed godwit, so-called because of their call

yava

noun
an alcoholic drink made from the roots of the Polynesian shrub *Piper methysticum*
  ❧ This is a variant spelling of 'kava'.

yaw
noun
the rotational movement or oscillation of a aircraft or spacecraft about a vertical axis

yerk
noun
a jerk or kick; a blow
verb
1 to jerk; to kick or lash out suddenly
2 to strike or lash with a whip

yorgan
noun
a Turkish quilt

Zz

zaftig or zoftig
adjective
1 full-bosomed
2 having a full, shapely figure; buxom
> ✧ The word is derived from Yiddish *zaftik* 'juicy'.

zegedine
noun
a silver drinking cup
> ✧ The name of this type of cup is believed to be derived from Szegedin, a city in Hungary.

zelotypia
noun
1 jealousy
2 zeal that is excessive to the point of morbidity

zenana
noun
the part of the house in which women and girls are secluded in India and Iran
> ✧ The word is Persian, from *zan* 'woman'. The zenana corresponds to the harem of Arabic-speaking Muslim countries.

zendalet

noun

(in Venice) a type of shawl worn either over the head or over the shoulders

Zoilism

noun

unjust or carping criticism; detraction

> ❧ The word is derived from the name of the ancient Greek grammarian Zoilus, who was known for his bitter criticism of Homer, Plato and others.

zoonist

noun

someone who believes that nature as a whole or natural objects are living beings